HAMPTONS HAVENS

The Best of *Hamptons Cottages and Gardens*

The Editors of *Hamptons Cottages and Gardens*

Newell Turner · Lockhart Steele

Bulfinch Press

New York · Boston

Bulfinch Press

Time Warner Book Group
1271 Avenue of the Americas, New York, NY 10020
Visit our Web site at www.bulfinchpress.com

First Edition

HC&G
Hamptons Cottages and Gardens

Library of Congress Cataloging-in-Publication Data

Hamptons havens: the best of *Hamptons cottages and gardens*/The editors of *Hamptons cottages and gardens*.
    p. cm.
  ISBN 0-8212-6194-0
1.   Architecture, Domestic—New York (State)—Hamptons. 2.   Interior decoration—New York (State)—Hamptons. 3.   Gardens—New York (State)—Hamptons. 4.   Hamptons (N.Y.)—Buildings, structures, etc.   I. Hamptons cottages and gardens.
NA7235.N72H355 2005
728'.37'0974725—dc22

                                                            2004021613

Design by Hotfoot Studio and Jill Tashlik

PRINTED IN SINGAPORE

ACKNOWLEDGMENTS

Special thanks to the Bulfinch team that saw this book from concept to completion: our publisher, Jill Cohen, editor Kristen Schilo, and Eveline Chao. Thanks also to our agent, Alan Kaufman. Finally, very special thanks to the homeowners who graciously allowed us to feature their homes— and their talented architects and interior designers who inspired us with their designs.

CONTENTS

INTRODUCTION

English colonists first settled the East End of Long Island, New York, in the late 1600s. Blessed with a temperate climate, good soil, and an extensive coastline, a chain of villages—Southampton, East Hampton, and Sag Harbor — flourished on the bounty of the fields and the trade that arrived by sea. By the turn of the nineteenth century, wealthy residents of New York City discovered the South Fork, now fondly called the Hamptons, and summer colonists began building rambling second homes (or "summer cottages") along the coasts and astride the fields. ■ For decades, life in the Hamptons remained quiet, even with the seasonal swelling of the population. Given the area's proximity to New York City and its cultural affluence, the area began to attract artists and writers who found inspiration in the natural beauty and quality of life here. Smaller communities like Amagansett, Wainscott, Sagaponack, Bridgehampton, Springs, Water Mill, Quogue, and Westhampton began to draw the attention of more people looking for their own haven. Architects and designers followed wealthy clients. Businesspeople of every stripe followed artists looking for "the scene." And on and on, until the Hamptons became internationally known for its luxury lifestyles. ■ In May 2002, *Hamptons Cottages and Gardens (HC&G)* was launched as a luxury home and garden magazine for the area. Since the first summer cottages were built over a century ago, real estate, architecture, and interior design have been passions for many. Whether their home is a multiple-bedroom estate, a contemporary box, or a renovated barn, Hamptonites take great pride in how and where they live. ■ *Hamptons Havens* is a compendium of some of our favorite homes covered during our first two summers. *HC&G* believes that all interior design should have a strong sense of place in some shape, form, or fashion, but in the end, good design is universal.

Newell Turner
Editor in Chief
Hamptons Cottages and Gardens

By the Sea

"A Thing of Beauty" by Amy Gross

I have the average New Yorker's contempt for the same-old, same-old, yet I'm always awed at the Constable-like arrangement of pond, trees, and meadow just west of the Maidstone Club in East Hampton. I'm in a house on Three Mile Harbor and I wake up to the sight of sailboats and their masts reflected in water, sometimes in mist, other times blindingly sunstruck. The image stuns me, day after day. The wild-armed junipers and walls of arborvitae, the grandeur of copper beeches near the pond, the ghostly santolinas and lavenders, and let's not even start with the wisteria . . . I eat all with my eyes. Or try to. I want to devour these images, memorize them, own them, and I can't. The beautiful thing is ungraspable, unmasterable, unendingly tantalizing. In front of a great painting in a foreign city — say one of Cézanne's Bathers *in Paris — I think: I have to remember the colors because reproductions never get it right and nothing but the original has the force that is pinning me to this spot. The same frustration — an exquisite frustration — can make watching dance painful: It will never be this way again and that's somehow tragic. The two — exquisite and tragic — get very close in beauty. It's all passing and it's perfect. It floods the screen of your mind — it overflows your heart.*

Beauty in a person is more complicated. If you were to walk through a garden and suddenly come upon a fat, fresh peony, it would startle its way into your attention — it would insist — and you could stare back freely and move on. Beauty in a person is just as startling, but staring dumbly is usually not allowed. Beauty in a person is confusing.

But there's another kind of human beauty that doesn't derive from physical equipment. In fact, I don't know its source, but it comes through a person's smile or eyes as radiant energy, aliveness, attention. It jumps the gap between the two of you. It melts all those crispy interior walls. And that's the link between you and anything beautiful — face, hedge, or house. It lifts you out of yourself, wakes you up, absorbs you, suffuses you with appreciation — which is pretty much my working definition of happiness.

10 ■

Amy Gross is an editor and a writer. She lives on Three Mile Harbor and in New York City.

Dune Maneuvers

On the Beach in Quogue, a former World War I Navy recreation hall is transformed into the ultimate sand-between-the-toes weekend retreat.

An aroma, one of nature's most evocative, is found in some homes along the Atlantic. It is a salty smell, an air of wood mixed with the sea, which summons spirits of summers past. This aroma cannot be bought or imported; it occurs only in homes that have stood for a generation or more. It is an aroma that must be earned. ■ In houses with this aura, you'll often find similar traits — kitchen floors with patterns of paths worn into them, claw-footed bathtubs, and screen doors that thud shut, having long since lost the desire to slam. These houses share something magical, too. It's the same relief an out-of-town visitor feels on arriving at a place where relaxation is the order of the day. In these houses it comes effortlessly, as well. ■ Step into the kitchen of the Dune Road house that Rick Livingston shares with his partner of twenty years, Jim Brawders, and you'll smell the aroma.

Opposite: Apple picking ladders flank the entrance to the middle bedroom. This page: "We call it the maid's room," Rick Livingston says of the guest bedroom by the kitchen. "Some guests say there's a childlike innocence to the room."

Opposite: The master bedroom looks out onto the dunes and to the ocean beyond. Below left: The dining area, at one end of the main room, includes a picnic table, an obelisk of shells, and a giant sponge. Below right: Sunlight pours into the main room through the skylight. Wicker furniture discovered in a barn upstate creates a casual sitting area.

Their Quogue summer retreat shares the other noted characteristics, but walking from the kitchen into the giant main room for the first time reduces details to mere footnotes. It is summer, and the laptop you brought will stay in its bag this weekend.

The place feels like the ultimate summer share house, with good reason. Livingston, an interior decorator with his own design firm, Period, in Manhattan, and Brawders, a senior vice president with the Corcoran Group real estate firm, were introduced to the house as members of a summer share in the early 1980s. That began their love affair with the home they call Sea Drift. The place gives the impression that it just swept in on the tide one night. And, in a sense, it did. Built as a recreation hall for Navy personnel during World War I, the structure was brought from Delaware by train in 1919. It arrived on flatbed cars at the local depot, then came by

■ 15

Below: Brawders pilots his '73 Mustang, with Livingston along for the ride. Right: Brawders' collection of crabs from the beach marches toward the sitting area on the back porch. Opposite: The bright red, 1953 stove discovered by Livingston stars in the kitchen.

horse-drawn wagon to the dune's edge in Quogue. Once in place, floorboards, gables, and studs were fitted back together like a jigsaw puzzle.

The house—a twenty-six-hundred-square-foot, barn-like structure with four bedrooms, two bathrooms, a kitchen, and an enormous, airy living room long ago carved out of the open interior—has stayed intact over the years, surviving fierce storms such as the hurricane of 1938. Neighboring structures were reduced to kindling. Though rising dunes have eliminated the ocean view, the sound of the crashing surf infuses the home with the rhythm of the beach.

Livingston, an avid antique treasure hunter, sought to echo the "found" quality of the original decor. His first great discovery was the red 1953 chamber stove. It had previously been the property of an old woman in Maine. In subsequent forays, he found wicker furniture (to replace a set that they didn't get to keep), the rope chandelier that now hangs in the center of the main room (and, separately, its tassels), and many of the home's nautical artifacts. Model ocean liners occupy tables in the main room, a result of Brawders' fascination with trans-Atlantic culture of the early twentieth century.

The three bedrooms aligned along one side of the house have their own personalities. The closet door in the master bedroom dances with vintage postcards, while wooden shutters line the middle bedroom. The corner bedroom is bathed

Opposite: Early maps in the middle bedroom show Long Island in 1910 and Quogue in the 1890s. Below left: A Styrofoam sandcastle sits near the master bathroom — its door framed with tantalizing murals. Below right: Wooden planks lead to a sitting area atop the dunes.

in sand tones. This variety is another part of the style that makes visitors to the house feel like they've relaxed there a thousand times before.

Sea air lures visitors outside to the back porch for morning coffee or to the front porch, tucked behind the dunes, for dinner. A seating area atop the dunes looks down to the beach and out across the sea. It's no surprise that, as Livingston says, "people who come here don't want to leave." This house is about summer as it was lived at an earlier time — and how it is still lived by a lucky few. Turn off the cell phone and soak up the atmosphere before Sunday afternoon comes again.

■ 19

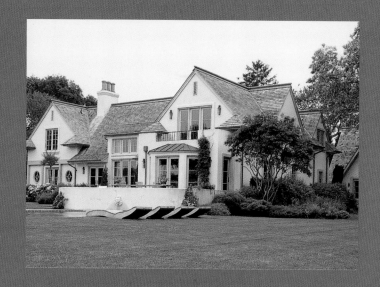

CHEZ GINSBERG

Working with a team of talented designers, a Water Mill couple takes a ranch house on Mecox Bay and transforms it into a little piece of the Old World.

You can tell by the gate at the entrance to the property that this place is different. While a nondescript, white picket fence fronts a neighbor's place, Joan and Frank Ginsberg have a beautiful, delicately wrought, iron gate that suggests a fairy-tale house lies beyond — one from a dreamy French fairy tale, that is. ■ A long, narrow driveway gently curves between thick hedges, giving the house a psychological distance from neighbors and the rest of the world. On a lovely bit of Mecox Bay in Water Mill, facing a courtyard of rose-colored cobblestones, is a vision that is more Normandy than Long Island. One could hardly guess it was born as a lowly ranch house. ■ "I bought it because of the property," Joan Ginsberg recalls.

Opposite: The house as seen from Mecox Bay.
This page: A courtyard welcomes visitors.
Three types of pavers were used to give
texture and history to the design.

Left: Rustic beams were added and left exposed in the drawing room. Above: The entrance has front-door grilles and iron detailing by John Battle of Battle Iron & Bronze.

"A friend of mine had seen it and said to me, 'You'll want it.' So I raced over there, and it was the most awful house I had ever seen! But then I went to the back. . . ."

Though the building is not large, every inch has been scrupulously decorated. At the same time, the Ginsbergs wanted a house they could walk into with bare, sandy feet. "They did not want the traditional Hamptons thing, but an Italian or French country-style place that was ultimately casual," says José Solís Betancourt, whose Washington-based interior design firm orchestrated the project.

Betancourt began the transformation by "adding some architecture," he says. Instead of simply slapping on extraneous elements, he thickened the walls and added a second story with a distinctive, low-sloping roof. He replaced interior plaster arches with rough wood lintels.

Ultimately, the unifying element is a very sophisticated and specific palette. Calling herself a "no-color person,"

■ 23

Ginsberg explains, "I wanted it to be about the water, but I
didn't want anything darker than the bay and landscape outside," she explains.

The walls, according to Paul Sherrill (who worked with
Betancourt on the interiors), sport subtle gradations of gray,
beige, and violet to mesmerizing effect. "The walls are made
of pigmented plaster layers," he points out.

As for the decor, "nothing sticks out," says Betancourt,
who can trace his penchant for mixing traditional and modern
to the influence of his mentor, John Saladino. Everywhere,
tablescapes and vignettes are placed just so. On a table of
perfectly aged wood, a bowl of bright green limes — two cut
and artfully arranged — add a controlled splash of color.

The Ginsbergs and the designers did much of the shopping
together. A favorite find was a pair of opera chairs for the
guest bedroom. "There's a hinge in the back, and women
would use them with the back flipped down like a stool so
they could put their hoop skirts right over the seat," Joan
explains.

Stone played a big part in the conception of a European
country typology. The couple even discovered a dealer of
period stone sinks, and they made the fixtures central to the
bathroom designs. "The sinks are from European mansions
in Istanbul," antiquarian Ani Antreasyan explains. "The

Below left: The bed in the master bedroom floats in the space facing French doors, which open to a view of Mecox Bay. Below right: The spacious master bathroom has a curtained niche for the tub. Opposite: A window seat in the master bedroom beckons, with throw pillows dressed in Old World Weavers' Chambord fabric.

rectangular ones usually came from laundry rooms, while the round or more decorated ones [are] from baths." They are naturally weathered by water and air.

The garden is no less charming. Landscape designer John (Jack) deLashmet used antique cobblestones and rustic pavers for a path that gradually "breaks apart" and disappears into the lawn in front of the guest cottage. "We wanted to create the feeling that nothing had been done to the landscaping for years," he says. On the other side of the house, deLashmet planted an olive grove.

DeLashmet sums up the basic challenge: "Ideally, we wanted to do Southern France and Italy meets Water Mill," he says. Because of the bay, deLashmet wanted the back of the house to feel more Water Mill than Europe. "The property needed to be embedded into the larger landscape. I see France winning out (slightly on the entrance side), with Water Mill as the victor on the water side — both sides living in an elegantly scruffy harmony."

ABOVE THE
MADDENING CROWDS

*Architect Fred Stelle crafts a retreat among the clouds
on Shelter Island's Divinity Hill.*

The Shelter Island house belonging to Sherry and Robert Wolfang just might have the best views on eastern Long Island. Sweeping panoramas of the North Fork, Peconic Bay, Long Island Sound, and Connecticut are so spectacular that the site, Divinity Hill, is aptly named. This place is indeed divine; not only in the sense of "oh, how divine," but also in its distinctive sense of otherworldliness. Here, the air, the light, the very atmosphere feel celestial. Clouds floating by overhead appear within reach, and sunsets are cinematic events. At an elevation of 162 feet, it is one of the highest points on Shelter Island. ■ "We bought

Opposite: Hints of the dramatic view beckon through the foyer at dusk. This page: A glass stairwell helps flood the Wolfangs' home with light.

Below left: In the master bedroom, a tub features a view of the North Fork. A Himalayan wool and silk carpet by Stephanie Odegard is soft underfoot. Below right: The kitchen glows in the late afternoon light of the Shelter Island sun. Opposite: The pool follows the graphic lines of the architecture along the side of the house and the curvaceous lines of the hillside on the other. Pillows in a green Donghia fabric pick up the colors of the surrounding landscape.

the view," the couple says, recalling their first visit back in 1988. The view, however, came with an interesting modernist house that possessed its own virtues and challenges. Designed by Peter Schladermundt, a major architect and industrial designer of the time, the house was quite avant-garde when it was built in the early 1960s. Like many houses of that genre — built to be interesting but modest —after some time it no longer best served the needs of its occupants.

The Wolfangs lived in the house for ten years before hiring Stelle Architects, in Bridgehampton, for a foundation-up renovation. "We knew Fred Stelle would keep the integrity of

the original house and expand it, open it to the view," Robert says.

The Wolfangs were ready for upgrades. For Sherry, who is a gourmet cook, a state-of-the-art kitchen was in order. Another big challenge was a corner in the living room, which interrupted the spectacular view. "All we thought about for ten years was how to eliminate the corner wall," Sherry adds.

Stelle Architects was cognizant of the attributes of the existing house, but a total renovation was necessary. "We were not haphazard in our efforts; we didn't want to get rid of the building," explains project architect Michael Lomont.

30 ■

Opposite & below: A jaw-dropping panorama of the North Fork is visible from the living room. Lead crystal table lamps by Thad Hayes for Boyd Lighting add a touch of glamour. Left: The scene at poolside.

Instead, the spirit of what was good about the original house was kept and incorporated into the new house.

The thirteen-hundred-square-foot house evolved in Stelle's mind into four thousand square feet spread across three levels, with Schladermundt's original footprint serving as a starting point. Stelle's new concept — two volumes joined by a glass pavilion — utilizes a few select materials in elegant ways. The anchor of the house, the stucco section, is detailed to look like a concrete box with a two-storied translucent corner of nineteen-foot-tall, acid-etched windows. Facing the street, it serves as a beacon in the surrounding woods, especially at night.

A delicate open steel and bluestone stairway provides graceful ascent to the master bedroom. Here, in an aerie above the treetops, is ultimate privacy. Fronting the view, a pavilion is wrapped in nine-foot-high walls of glass that span from floor to ceiling — nothing obstructs the view. Furnishings are kept spare and low, so they virtually disappear. Neutral hues allow nature's changing palette to color the room fresh from season to season.

The seamless indoor/outdoor flow of the house was achieved through the use of consistent materials. "We like to complement rather than intrude on the landscape," says Stelle, who favors simple materials — stone, steel, and glass

Below: The billiard room sports a Don chair and ottoman by Gerard Von Berg from Boltax Gallery. Right: Sunlight filters through a glass-encased steam shower in the bathroom. Opposite: A Chinese elm root from Roark takes center stage during summer on the living room hearth. The Saarinen Tulip table is from Laurin Copen Antiques. The tray and tumblers are from In Home.

used in a pure way. "This is a common thread in our work — letting each material have its own identity and integrity," the architect explains.

Using twenty-first-century structural capabilities and products like anodized aluminum windows and doors, the house is designed to be low maintenance and cost efficient. Radiant heat under the stone tile entry and kitchen floors is steady and foot warming on cold days.

"We didn't build this kind of house to be pretentious. We did it for our lifestyle," Robert says. He wanted extreme privacy, and Sherry wanted a house with a water view. For them, having achieved this with such architectural perfection, the house is thrilling. "I never take it for granted," Sherry says. "I am still stopped dead in my tracks when I come in here, and my heart beats a little faster."

AN ENDLESS SUMMER

One of a few structures to survive the legendary hurricane of 1938,
Kilkare has become an icon on the East Hampton beach.

High on a dune above the Atlantic and Georgica Pond, Kilkare stands sentry. For generations it has served as a landmark for passing ships and legions of beachgoers. Hurricanes
have left their mark, but years of weather have given the house a priceless patina. ■ Inside,
time seems to stand still. Sunlight filtering through screened doors and salt-tinted windows
gives the rooms the quality of a faded photograph. Constructed by shipbuilders in the nineteenth century, Kilkare currently plays host to Eleanore and Michael Kennedy, their family,
and a multitude of friends. "The house is still protected by the ghosts of the original owners, Camilla and Jonathan Edwards," says Eleanore Kennedy. "They appear each year. They
protect the house; they protect the family." ■ The Kennedys first fell in love with Kilkare

Opposite: Constructed by shipbuilders in 1879, Kilkare occupies a bluff on Georgica Pond in East Hampton — one of the most stunning, and familiar, promontories in the Hamptons. Below: For the fireplace in the dining room — one of nine fireplaces in the house — a collection of shells decorates the mantel. Besides serving as decorative icons, the shells on the mantel double as place cards. Once a meal is complete, guests' shells join the pile, awaiting each person's eventual return.

nearly three decades ago, when they spotted it in a magazine ad that read, "A Gift from the Sea." It was extremely run down and showed its age, having suffered wind and water damage during its vacancy — not to mention a century's worth of sea air. But as Eleanore Kennedy explains, "It was love at first sight. We were weak in the knees, and there was a spiritual connection. Nothing matters when you fall in love. You don't see the flaws. Later, when you see them, you acknowledge them and change them with love." The couple compassionately restored the house to its original state. "The house had great dignity; it had great bones," she adds. "What was accomplished was an exercise in restraint — absolute restraint."

Originally, Kilkare had no kitchen on the main floor, so the butler's bedroom was converted to accommodate present-day needs. Everything else in the house is as it was, yet lighter and brighter. The pine floors were stripped and stained a golden pumpkin color. The walls, whose plaster actually contains sand as an aggregate, were salvaged when possible. Nowhere is the beauty of the painstaking restoration more apparent than in the ceilings. Each room has a different ceiling pattern executed in thin strips of molding, so each had to be dismantled and re-created according to its original design.

Decor by restraint meant keeping many of the original furnishings and adding pieces only in keeping with the natural colorations of sand and earth. White natural hemp fabrics

Left: The hanging lamps in the master bedroom were originally in a schoolhouse. Here, they are hung for reading in bed. The bed and blanket rack are original to the house; both have been restored. Above: Sunlight spills onto the pumpkin-colored pine floor in the bedroom.

cover the caned and carved nineteenth-century, Anglo-Indian furniture in the living room. Tables by the legendary California designer John Dickinson add to the sense of timelessness, bridging ancient mythology with seventies modernism. The dining room table stretches the length of the room, accommodating the many guests who often sit down to dinner. Shells serve as place cards, and the dining room's white-washed mantel is a shrine to many good meals — it's piled deep with shells bearing the names of family and endless friends.

Upstairs, the bedrooms and bathrooms are painted the color of Long Island beach sand with pine paneling. The floors are perfectly bare. The warm summer breezes that move through the rooms ripple antique lace coverlets and

■ 41

shawls that are used to dress four-poster and wicker beds. Sunlight floods through partially open windows that are left unadorned save blackout shades that permit guests to sleep in late. The overall effect is "monastic in feeling, but truly liberating," Eleanore Kennedy explains. "It is a place where we can think and indulge ourselves in nature. The home we have created is always about the views and the sea."

Kilkare epitomizes summer. Georgica Pond, Eleanore Kennedy says, is "where our children were raised, friendships nurtured, and milestones celebrated. All is in harmony." A peace symbol made of stones at the base of the flagpole says it all. The love of life that the Kennedy family cherishes will always be part of this beloved house. The laughter of family and friends will be the sounds of future ghosts that join the Edwards family in the centuries to come.

Above: A banquette looks out to the beach and sea beyond.
Opposite: The living room is the epitome of beachside living. Raj furniture, including a daybed, plays against animal-footed plaster tables by the late California designer John Dickinson. The fabric of choice is "industrial" hemp, chosen for its mildew resistance. A whitewashed rack of elk horns, from the mountains of New Mexico, occupies pride of place on the chimney.

SPELLBOUND

High on a bluff above Shinnecock Bay, Betty Wasserman works her magic on an estate house built at the turn of the last century.

"When clients ask me if they can have color," says interior designer Betty Wasserman, "I tell them neutrals, greens, and lavender. Baby blue is okay. It's livable." Confident and decisive, Wasserman's prescription for a client's second home in Hampton Bays has transformed a down-at-the-heels estate house into a glamorous, yet perfectly relaxed, beachside home. ■ After helping her friend and client with a town house in the city, Wasserman was asked to take a look at this hulking brick house and make some suggestions to resolve a heating problem in the master bedroom on the second floor. Like most perfectionists, Wasserman started with a handful of ideas that led to her re-dressing the house from top to bottom. "I also knew that she needed to expand the kitchen," Wasserman explains. "Two meetings later

Opposite: Horse–head statues command the entrance to the house. This page: A thirty-eight-foot-long custom rug by Odegard begins in the foyer and guides guests to the living room. Beneath the stairs, a barn-like door suspended from a glider rail leads to the kitchen.

Opposite: A John Wigmore light sculpture floats above the living room mantel. Holly Hunt sofas, a Chris Lehrecke daybed, and cowhide-covered ottomans amplify comfort. Left: Casual dining in the solarium is heightened by vases and a centerpiece bowl from H Groome. The silk curtains are in Ivy by Donghia. Below: A chair and ottoman are silhouetted against a bettyhome bamboo media cabinet.

we were gutting the whole house. This investment banker did everything the right way."

Originally, all of the rooms were bright white, and the floors were orange. "My client had bought the house furnished eight years earlier and had been living in it as it was," Wasserman says. "The real challenge was staying true to some of the original details, like the coffered ceiling, but allowing it to move into a modern look and feel."

More than at any show house, this house is a place to take out a notebook and study the details. Decorating lessons can be found through every door.

"Believe it or not, the previous furniture in the living room was too big," Wasserman says. Still, she has managed to gracefully arrange the room with three sofas, a daybed, a number of commodious armchairs, an enormous cocktail table, and a pair of furry ottomans. "This room was too big for one seating plan, but not big enough for two," Wasserman explains. The solution was for two opium bed–style sofas by Christian Liagre and an equally sizable daybed to corral the cocktail table in front of the fireplace.

In the dining room, Wasserman started with an antique dining table that her client brought to the East End from England. She surrounded it with slim dining chairs and filled in the corners of the room with low, comfortable armchairs.

Like a style arbiter who knows how to combine vintage clothing with new clothes, Wasserman understands how to mix and match the furniture in her rooms for a look that is very individual. Scale and quality are the keys to playing this game.

For years Wasserman's client had really lived in only a small portion of the house. The kitchen, for one, was way too small and completely inefficient, with refrigerators occupying an enclosed back porch. This room underwent the most reconstruction, with the help of architect Glenn Leitch. Wasserman and her client wanted a kitchen with a clean and inviting design for entertaining friends and literally dining in that was also substantial enough and professionally arranged to accommodate catering teams for large affairs.

In every room of the house, Wasserman makes a statement through understatement. Yards and yards of fabric — not just any fabric, but a lush, ivy green Donghia silk — line the walls and windows of a more casual dining room in the old solarium. The curtain walls hide unused doorways and

Above: The curtain fabric and Murano glass lamp are from Donghia. Club chairs in the corners help fill the large room and give the dining room additional functions. Opposite: A spacious kitchen makes entertaining here a pleasure. A blackened steel fireplace with raised hearth adds warmth in the evening. An Urban Archaeology light fixture illuminates the beautiful sandstone surface of the island.

48 ■

Opposite: The bed is dressed with Calvin Klein Home linens, decorative pillows in Larsen fabric, and an Anichini throw for cool evenings. Photographs of the ocean by Tom Baril hang above the bed in the master bedroom. Below left: The grand master bathroom is divided into wet and dry areas by a glass wall. The azul marble subway and Chiclet tiles line the room, which also sports a pair of King Kong–size showerheads from Waterworks. The bathtub is original to the house. Below right: A Holly Hunt Cyclades chair, upholstered in a Donghia fabric, anchors a woven grass rug from Williams-Sonoma.

warm up a room that is otherwise chilly from the breezes off the bay. The master bathroom is sheathed (walls and floor) in a blue marble with a glass wall separating the wet and dry areas. No bubble-spewing jet sprays are needed to enhance the bathing experience, just a deep, white, cast-iron tub placed meditatively beneath a window.

Everyone has some degree of design sensibility, but the help of a professional can never hurt. Designing a room is not so dissimilar from smart dressing. The goal is to look good but not too studied — just like the rooms in this house, simply stunning.

51

BAY WATCH

*An artist in search of a waterfront property finds a
magical glen with a house waiting to be saved.*

Properties once existed on the South Fork that real-estate brokers didn't bother showing

people — houses in need of so much TLC that they scared away most potential homeowners.

(Sound like a dream or a fairy tale?) But as recently as the early 1990s, some gems were still

hidden away in the Hamptons waiting to be discovered — places waiting for that buyer

with just a little cash and a lot of vision to notice the potential. Maybe it wasn't South of

the Highway or along the ocean or in a village, but miles of land along the bays harbored

plenty of waterfront opportunities. ■ "At that time, no one had heard of Noyack," claims

an artist who for years had been splitting her time between a house in Bridgehampton and

a Greenwich Village town house. "It was kind of like Brooklyn." Realizing that she really

Opposite: A contorted beech tree gets the specimen treatment and anchors the cottage garden with the stone stairs that lead up a hill to the swimming pool. This page: Beach plum, Rosa rugosa, sumac, grasses, heather, and "lots of tough stuff that could take the wind" (in the words of Jack deLashmet) were planted in and along the stone wall that supports the gazebo at this Noyack house.

Left: Tall vertical windows open the living room to the garden, and the homeowner added a pair of double doors to open the view to the sunroom and the bay beyond.

wanted to live on the water, though, she turned to a broker, who finally said, "I'm going to show you some stuff they don't even show."

As they turned off Noyack Road into a newly divided suburban neighborhood, the broker added, "People avoid this property like the plague."

The artist in this client had her doubts. But as the driveway became a bumpy dirt road winding down a ravine, "you really felt like you were in the country," she recalls. Even better, at the end sat a falling-down house with spectacular frontage on Little Peconic Bay.

"Beyond scary," she says. "It was truly a wreck." Originally, it had been a barn moved to the site sometime before the 1920s and converted into a summerhouse. Since then, it had been used as a boys' camp and most recently served as the residence of a religious group. "Bible verses were painted on the walls, and words about ascending to heaven were painted on the stairs," the artist recalls.

■ 55

Below: The homeowner and deLashmet decided to place the swimming pool on the top of one of the hills that border the ravine, where it also provides a fantastic view of Little Peconic Bay. Right: Everyone questioned the practicality of a six-by-six-foot lounge mounted permanently on the house. But, during the day, it is a sunny invitation to enjoy the water view, and at night, it becomes an observatory to watch the stars above the bay. Opposite: A new gazebo, based on designs from the 1920s, replaced an older one that was moved up the glen to a vegetable garden.

Now a red-and-blue map painted on the wall of the sun-porch (which had been completely blacked out with Sheetrock) is the only trace of those occupants. The artist and single mother has transformed it into a summerhouse again — more evocative than it probably ever was before. Her builder said it was a money pit. Architect after architect said tear it down. But a lot can be said for the artist's eye in the world of real estate. With a sensitivity for details and recognizing beauty in the quirks of what already existed, her meticulous renovation literally breathed life back into the house.

"She's got such an incredible sense of unerring taste," adds her friend and noted landscape designer John (Jack) deLashmet. "Everyone forgets time there. It's magical." But, in the beginning, the grounds were as much a disaster as the house. "There was no place to walk or sit anywhere outside," deLashmet explains. "It was just one big ravine." Recommended to the homeowner by mutual friends, "we hit it off absolutely immediately. Our vocabulary is the same. Our sensitivity is the same," he says about their budding friendship and collaboration on the gardens. "We wanted it to look like everything had been there forever. She definitely didn't want to over-landscape it." They decided to keep things natural and native, and when something was used that wasn't exactly native, they would "toss a few up into the woods" to blur the boundaries.

Around the entrance to the house, they organized a small, more formal cottage garden.

Hearing the homeowner describe the process of renovation makes it sounds easy, even to the uninitiated. "I've been doing houses for twenty years," she says. "I've always found old, funky things and cleaned them up." In the end, though, it takes more than desire to create a home for the present that is also this comfortable with the past. It takes an artist's eye.

■ 59

GILDING THE LILY

In a home on Lily Pond Lane in East Hampton, designer
Kristin Hein eschews stuffiness for livability.

With expansive lawns and even more expansive homes, Lily Pond Lane is one of the most gracious stretches in East Hampton. The majestic homes are stately — some might even say imposing — which is exactly what the owners of one of this street's most impressive homes didn't desire. "They wanted their home to be user-friendly," says Kristin Hein, the designer who recently redecorated the interiors. "There's an amazing spirit about the family. They didn't want a stuffy design. The family loves to laugh and entertain. It is supposed to be a place where the daughters feel comfortable coming in wearing their bikinis and carrying a margarita." ■ Could that concept translate to this setting? Having moved to the South Fork several years ago with her business partner, Philip Cozzi, Hein became fascinated by

Opposite: The house occupies a prominent site on the dunes along Lily Pond Lane. This page: Throughout the house, decorator Kristin Hein chose colors that relate to both the art in each room and the outdoors. In the living room, she outfitted 1940s Italian chairs from Gray Gardens, Bridgehampton, in a pale fabric by Groves Brothers. The French 1930s mirrored-top coffee table, found at Mecox Gardens, Bridgehampton, has carved deer-hoof-shaped feet. The English ceramic platter is from Bloom, Sag Harbor.

Left: In the living room, sofas made of cerused teak from British Khaki are upholstered in the company's Natural Linen. Large floor cushions and pillows are upholstered in Groves Brothers hand-silkscreened fabric, available at Old World Weavers. The cocktail table is from Mecox Gardens. Above: The dining room is painted the color of wet sand.

this sprawling 1920s house set high on a bluff overlooking the ocean, with a grand, Gatsbyesque lawn stretching from the street to the dunes.

The family of Reginald Lewis, the late CEO of Beatrice Foods, felt the same way. Though the family had a home in Amagansett, they would routinely drive past this extraordinary structure. "One of the daughters," Hein says, "told me her father loved the house and would always kid them, saying, 'That's where Daddy Warbucks lives.'" When the Lewises' Amagansett home was destroyed by fire, they attempted to buy the East Hampton house, but negotiations fell through. Reginald Lewis passed away shortly afterward, but his wife, a Philippines-born lawyer, was determined to see his dream fulfilled. In a short time Loida Lewis and her two teenage daughters, Leslie and Christina, finally moved in.

Last year, when it was time to redo the interiors of the seven-bedroom house following major renovations, Lewis called on Hein. The project posed several challenges. One

■ 63

was time. It was February, and the house needed to be ready for Memorial Day. Another obstacle could have been that Lewis was traveling much of the time, but Christina was available to act as a sounding board and facilitate quick decisions.

"The jumping-off point for the design was the amazing surroundings of the ocean, the green grass, and the quality of changing light," Hein says. "I wanted to bring the outdoors in." That meant window coverings were kept to a minimum. "Where there were going to be curtains, I wanted to have gorgeous sheer fabric just blowing in the breeze."

The landscape, though, was not the only inspiration Hein was given. For years the family had possessed a notable art collection, lovingly nurtured by Reginald Lewis. Hein, who has a background in art history, was delighted. "They have great Cubist art, African-American art . . . wonderful paintings and sculptures. When I got the transparencies, I was like a kid in a candy store." Incorporating a collection into any home is a challenge, but making it an organic part of a beach house was especially tricky.

Above: A pool table contributes to the home's relaxed feel. Opposite: Pale green pervades the sunroom. Whimsical touches include an African fertility sculpture set in the corner. The black wicker sofa and chairs are from Janus et Cie.

64 ■

Below: A dresser from Laurin Copen Antiques offsets a Napoléon III chair from Schorr & Dobinsky. Right: A guest bedroom features classic twin beds with headboards in white canvas, sheer white curtains, and Philippe Starck's Louis Ghost chair, in the foreground. Opposite: Another bedroom features bedding from the Elegant John. The painted iron étagère, with milk-glass shelves and wicker decoration, and the zinc lamps are both from Gray Gardens.

Blending the art into the home seamlessly was achieved, in part, through the unifying element of color. "The Lewises and I are all color addicts," Hein confesses. "We didn't want there to be any white walls." Throughout the house color is used liberally, borrowing palettes from the art and the surrounding grass, sand, sea, and, most important of all, sky. The rooms are all different — persimmon, lavender, pale yellow — each linked to the art and the colors outside. The dining room, for example, is the color of wet sand.

Furnishings are simple. In most instances, Hein started fresh, purchasing pieces from local resources. Most sought-after were items that would echo the natural elements. "I like using indigenous materials, so I found things like teak dining chairs that almost feel like driftwood just rolled into the house. We were looking for a kind of barefoot elegance."

Hein knew that her clients wanted a place that would welcome many generations of guests, so she left the rooms open and airy, with touches like window seats for accommodating an overflow of visitors. From the outside, the house may look grand and imposing, but on the inside there are people having a good time, with sandy feet and wet bathing suits — and maybe even a margarita in hand.

VERNER PANTON

JAPONISME

Gio Ponti

Mark Rothko

The Art of Bloomsbury

ART NOUVEAU 1890-1914

LE LIVRE DU BAIN

ANDREE PUTMAN

MAXINE OLD

IN THE VILLAGE

"ON MY BIKE" BY SPALDING GRAY

Now I'm riding past the historic cemetery on my left, to turn right on Jermain Ave. And ride by the other cemetery, Oakland Cemetery. How I love these cemeteries. They are such great negative spaces and it's nice to be almost sure that the greedy contractors can't develop there. Now I am riding past a duck pond on my right and headed for the intersection of Main Street and Brick Kiln Road. I ride through the traffic light, which takes me very quickly out of the historic village of Sag Harbor and into the hodgepodge of crazy, mixed-up architecture. I pass the fire station on my right which gives me a clear view of my first American flag of the day, which tells me in its colorful way that we have a healthy northwest wind.

Then all of the sudden, POW! I'm out and riding along the water and shock-a-roo! It's a million-dollar view! It's all a glorious out-of-season Caribbean blue! Now that northwest wind is behind me and driving me on as my head opens up over the bay. Seagulls hover and soar and that old familiar smell of autumn mixed with brine enters and fills me. I am riding fast and smooth now with the brilliant energizing bay on my left, then out of Long Beach parking lot, I ride onto Route 114. And coming in for my final run as I pass the North Haven Settlement sign, which reads "settled in 1664."

Now for the final homestretch, I ride up onto the bridge that spans the channel of water that separates Sag Harbor from North Haven. When I get to the center of the bridge, I stop. There in the middle of the bridge I am up high enough to have an overview of the town. Beyond the cove I see the long wharf, where the whaling ships used to come in. I see another American flag blowing and I see the harbor with its elegant sailboats. Then I see the breakwater and the bay beyond. In the distance I see the nature conservancy on Shelter Island. It is so lovely to see such undeveloped land all stretching out in that autumn, purplish rusty hue.

To my right I see what looks like a sort of medieval wall of motel, condos, two professional buildings, and three restaurants, all surrounding the village, which peeks up behind them like a *pop-up card with old colonial brick-and-clapboard Victorians, and all its churches. Then, in a ludicrous way, as if put there to save the town from becoming a piece of generic calendar art, there sits a big blue one-hundred-foot-high natural-gas ball. It looks like a giant pool ball that has just rolled into town and come to rest.*

I love this little overview and I think, as I stand on that bridge, I wish the town had a little hill I could climb up and look back down from. I would love to climb up a hill just to get that godly distance on it all, just to have that overview. Once, I did have a God's-eye overview, when I was flying back from London with my family in a giant 747. We flew right over Sag Harbor in the daylight and we all looked down at the Whaler's Church, at our house and the long wharf. It was a true God's-eye view and all of Sag Harbor looked like a Norman Rockwell Monopoly town. It was just nestled there with its off-season population of 2009, about the size of the population of an average New York City subway at rush hour.

The late Spalding Gray, a noted writer, actor, and performer, was a longtime resident of Sag Harbor.

BUILDING WITH THE PAST

An antiques dealer who treasures provenance fills a reproduction Colonial house with vintage furnishings from her extensive collections.

When you go to a Hamptons antiques store, you can be sure everything has a story ("this came from so-and-so's third wife's second house, who bought it from such-and-such"). With Jean Sinenberg — who since the early 1970s has operated three stores in the area and who also organizes eight antiques shows every summer — everything that touches her life has a tale to tell. "This bracelet," she says, extending a wrist adorned in pink and yellow-gold links, "is from Pat Funt's. She has a shop in Darien, and she comes to my shows. She is the daughter of Alan Funt, the *Candid Camera* man. A lovely family." ■ Sinenberg can't

Opposite: Antiques set the tone at Jean Sinenberg's home. This page: Beautifully weathered wooden doors lead to a treasure trove of antiques — many collected, others passed down to collector and dealer Sinenberg.

Opposite: American wicker from Ted Meyer's Harbor Antiques fills the veranda. Above: The house is a convincing Colonial reproduction. Windsor chairs from the Northeast surround the dining table. The 1840s grandfather clock was found early in the career of the dealer.

resist buying the occasional bauble for her own shop. But jewelry is just a tiny part of the vast mix at the sprawling complex that is Georgica Creek Antiques, in Wainscott. Here is a lamp with brass monkeys, there is an ornamental birdcage; you can find old riding boots, an oval desk completely covered in embossed leather, a marble fireplace surround, and important china. Almost all of her current inventory comes from local residences, so it is always unpredictable. The same can be said of Sinenberg's house.

Though the Hamptons are filled with lovely old homes, Sinenberg "imported" Lloyd A. Kirley, an architect from Massachusetts who specializes in restorations and reproductions. He built a copy of a house in Deerfield, Connecticut — although Sinenberg has never seen the original — with only a few departures from the model. "We wanted a nine-foot ceiling on the second floor, but the whole structure would have exceeded the maximum height for building around here,"

■ 75

Sinenberg explains. "We had to put a gambrel roof instead."

A few skylights add a modern touch, and in great contrast to the all-white facade and trim, the entrance is through a distinctive double door in weathered, honey-colored wood. "The doors were in my shop for a long time, but there were no takers, so I thought I'd use them," Sinenberg recalls.

A tour of the house is a learning experience. How do you spot a real Windsor chair? "The old Windsors have big pegs — these are eighteenth century," says Sinenberg of the ones around her dining table. "There is such a thing as fire-house Windsor, which is clunkier and sturdy but very nice, and usually made of oak. Those chairs were made later — manufactured — and they were used in a lot of firehouses. But true Windsors were hand carved and look more sculptural. As a dealer or collector, you develop a feeling of being able to relate. Sure, you look for certain technical things. But you have to sense the aesthetic."

Sinenberg also collects Canton pottery, which doesn't look as delicate as some other Chinese porcelain but is charming nonetheless. "Canton pieces were done by children in the

Above: Even the house's details are steeped in history. A Coromandel style screen stretches between two original eighteenth-century pillars. Below it sits a sofa from the Rubinstein estate. Opposite: Accessories from years of collecting include a decorative eighteenth-century mirror found at the Cyr Auction Company. Plucked from early-nineteenth-century weather vanes: a full-bodied rooster and cow. The sofa is 1850s English. Above the mantel is a collection of rare American redware.

76

Opposite: Books and unique furnishings, including two coveted rockers, occupy the library. In the foreground is an unusual gypsy willow rocker and beside it, a rocker made by the Dominy family of East Hampton. Left: A chair beckons in the master bedroom. Below: Furnishings from several centuries fit nicely together in the master bedroom. Atop the bedroom's four-poster bed is one of Sinenberg's first passions, an early American quilt. This folksy version is hand-sewn entirely in blue-and-white cottons.

1850s and 1860s," she explains. "They are very heavy and were used as ballast in ships that came here carrying silks. The pots would then also be sold." What about the Deco-looking white couch? "Well, that was in the shop for a while," she says. "It was attributed to Helena Rubinstein's estate through her nephew, who was selling things out of his house on Lily Pond Lane."

Off the living room is an ample screened porch filled with green wicker furniture. "I had it painted dark green," Sinenberg explains. "Originally it was mostly white. Some are Heywood Wakefield, from the late nineteenth century. They were very good wicker makers. Wicker is a very American phenomenon — nobody makes wicker like Americans. It's strong and holds up well." The upstairs rooms are filled with various treasures, including an unusual gypsy willow rocker ("I've had it since 1970 and have had countless friends and colleagues try to buy it."). A pretty bench in the master bedroom came from local dealer Court Talmage, whose ancestors were early settlers of East Hampton in the 1600s.

And the outsize tureen on the dining table? "It's actually an old English porcelain footbath," Sinenberg admits with a laugh. Now here is a woman who is not afraid of new table-top concepts.

RAINBOW IN A BOX

Benjamin Noriega-Ortiz turns a 1980s-era house into a fantasyland through the innovative use of color and shapes.

As advice goes, "think inside the box" doesn't sound like the greatest way to encourage inspiration. Yet that was the marching order given to decorator Benjamin Noriega-Ortiz by a married couple seeking a makeover of a flat-roofed box house in Quogue they'd recently purchased. ■ The decorator responded in out-of-the-box fashion, turning an unexceptional, early 1980s spec house into a dreamy fantasyland through the creative use of shape and color. In the process, he authored a lesson on how beauty can be achieved on a budget with a lot of vision — and a little patience. ■ Longtime Manhattanites Jessica Ushan and Ron Schecter found themselves drawn to a contemporary house despite their preconceived notions of what they would find in the Hamptons. "Initially we thought, Oh, an old shingle

Left: "I wanted to make the entry to the house more theatrical, so now you enter the house through drapery," says Noriega-Ortiz about the dramatic front entryway. The semisheer nylon drapes are custom made; the columns are from the clients' collection. Above: At the rear of the house, a swimming pool lures visitors.

house would be nice," Ushan recalls. "When we saw the light in a contemporary house, we changed our minds. This was a sunny house — and it looked like an easy one to manage."

The couple turned to Noriega-Ortiz to bring the same sense of flair to their Quogue house that he'd lavished on Ushan's Manhattan apartment and office. In the city, Ushan and Schecter were impressed with the decorator's use of a mostly monochromatic color palette to create an ethereal feeling of light in dark spaces. Now, confronted with a Hamptons house flooded with natural light, Noriega-Ortiz took a different approach, bathing each room of the house in a single, distinct rainbow color.

"When I went to see the house, I realized it's really a box," Noriega-Ortiz recalls. "It has a center living room area, like a courtyard, and rooms around it like you'll find in a Spanish house in my hometown of San Juan, Puerto Rico. We decided to make this 'courtyard' into a big entertaining

room. The surrounding rooms we'd do in individual colors —
that way, the house would look bigger."

Budget limitations restricted the homeowners to decorating one room at a time. So one by one, over a two-year
period, the rooms received their color christenings. The living room became a very pale blue, the master bedroom light
purple, and one of the three guest bedrooms an apple green.
Noriega-Ortiz's color concepts did not stop there. "It's an old
idea to do rooms by color, but we extended that to doing
things in the room with a hint of the color," he says. "Furniture often matches the respective wall color. There are no
patterns — I really dislike them. I use interesting shapes
instead. So this house is a study of shapes and colors."

84 ■

*Above left & opposite: The living
room features a mix of modern and
antique pieces. Custom feather-
shade lamps are by And Bob's Your
Uncle. The sofa is from Donghia.
The coffee table is from Far Eastern
Antiques. Ushan collects the white
glass that adorns a wall of the living room on eBay. Above right: The
plastic chair is by Steen Ostergaard
via eBay.*

Opposite: The master bedroom is a study in purples. Left & below: Vegetables overflow a bowl on the antique dining table. The dining area opens off the living room and faces the swimming pool. The photographs on the wall were taken by Schecter, an accomplished amateur photographer.

It is also a study in the dramatic. The house's front exterior is framed with giant, semisheer, nylon drapes. Inside, another set of translucent drapes blurs the reality of the living room beyond — where a final set of drapes separates the interior space from the swimming pool at the back of the house. "It is a great set to enter," Noriega-Ortiz notes. "I think of it as a layering of fantasy and reality."

The abundant sunlight toys with the colors in the house. "The living room can look white, but when the light changes, you feel the colors change," Ushan says. "I was having a debate with someone about the color of the fireplace — is it blue or purple? When you look from one room into another, the colors always look a little different against one another."

This transformative nature makes the house a literal dreamscape for its owners. "Once we're there, it actually feels like we're not in a house but somewhere in another land," Schecter marvels. "We weren't afraid to go with Benjamin's vision of what it could be, and thank goodness we did, because we believe it worked on every level."

LILLIPUTIAN MANOR

A renovation gives a big boost to an 1870s saltbox in East Hampton.

People often buy houses that are fixer-uppers, without a clear idea of who exactly will do the "fixing-upping." Not so with Brian del Toro and Jim Penny. From the moment they first saw their 1870s saltbox in East Hampton, they knew it was their own elbow grease that would give this timeworn cottage a new lease on life. ■ "It was partially a financial decision, but we also wanted to learn how to do things ourselves," says del Toro. ■ "Yes, but we nearly killed each other at the beginning," admits Penny, an executive recruiter. "We learned to pick our battles." ■ Both agree that del Toro initially had the clearer vision of how best to proceed. He is, after all, an interior designer who has had stays with Parish-Hadley, David Kleinberg, and Connie Beale, Inc. As many decorators are perplexed to discover, however, designing for others can be easier than designing for oneself. And del Toro

Opposite: Eyebrow windows were added to the front facade. This page: A vintage Haywood-Wakefield daybed — and a breeze through the window — make for ideal reading conditions.

Opposite: The sofa, covered in fabric from Scalamandré, commands the living room with style. Clarence House and Cowtan & Tout fabrics add pattern on the pillows and ottoman. The trim is from M & J Trimming Co. Left: The living room fireplace was cleverly repositioned during the renovation of the house. Below: A hammock swings in the backyard garden.

wanted to reflect not only his tastes but Penny's as well.

"So, I decided that I was the general contractor," he says, "and Jim was the client." Hearing this statement, Penny's eyes widen. "A client who relinquished control," he says, laughing merrily.

Enchanted by the house's simple, old-fashioned structure, the couple wanted to "keep it quiet and true to what it was," del Toro says. But only up to a point. For what it "was" had been a small, two-story, one-bathroom house where six children were raised. This meant teeny-tiny rooms, dropped ceilings, and floors covered by layers of linoleum, under which they found World War II–era newspapers.

Other than inserting eyebrow windows on the second floor, the biggest challenge was how to add a fireplace — a problem complicated by the furnace venting up through the original chimney. "This was a headache," del Toro allows. His clever solution was to design a new firebox in the living room on the same line as the staircase and balance this with a television cabinet constructed on the opposite side.

When it came time for bricklaying, rewiring, and plumbing — labors wisely relegated to professionals — the couple stayed busy with an ambitious landscaping project. They added a grapevine arbor and flowerbeds, built an outside shower, ripped out an asphalt driveway, stacked up stone walls and planted mountain laurel, hydrangea, and Rose of

Below left: Vintage pieces, including a tortoise shell and a Chinese cinnabar lamp, are arranged under a Swedish painting bought on eBay. Below right: The color theme carries through to the Frette linens, which are trimmed in red. Opposite: The William IV dining table, chairs, and American armoire, found at The Yard Sale, are all mahogany.

Sharon. Whew! "For the first year we owned the place, we didn't go to the beach once," Penny recalls.

It seems that Penny's role as client finally emerged when it came time for decorating. A graduate of the Merchant Marine Academy, he counts a wooden toy replica of the SS *United States*—launched in 1952 and still considered America's greatest ocean liner—among his cherished possessions. So, the master bedroom, a true boy's room, has a nautical theme with paintings of ships, a four-poster bed, and red plaid curtains (sewn by del Toro).

92 ■

Opposite: The painted wood bed is part of an antique bedroom set, again from The Yard Sale. The embroidered, vintage-looking pillowcases are from Anthropologie. Other linens are from Ralph Lauren Home. Left: A chair and dresser complete the light blue bedroom, which offers a nice contrast to the masculine master bedroom. Below: An antique American Federal wingback chair is covered in a Jacques Bouvet et Cie stripe. The eyebrow windows were added by del Toro.

Similarly evocative antiques are found throughout the house. Some are whimsical, like the guest bedroom's cottage furniture from the late nineteenth century. Others are surprisingly stately, such as a William IV breakfast table and an American Empire mahogany armoire in the dining room. Most were bought on eBay, at a Louisiana auction house, or at The Yard Sale.

"Our apartment in New York is slicker, and I suppose we wanted a respite from that," suggests del Toro. "But we didn't want it to look twee. After all, this is a weekend place, not a historical installation."

Thanks to their Herculean efforts, this cottage is also no longer a work in progress. Indeed, the men are even unapologetic about a squeaky staircase. "My dad gave us an article about how to fix that, but we kind of like it," Penny says. "It reminds us that we live in an old house."

HOUSE AND GARDENER

How a one-time graphic designer found his true calling in the soil of the South Fork, then put his talents to work on an old carriage house.

Nowadays, landscape designer Craig Socia has some of the South Fork's most prestigious gardens under his (green) thumb. That's the last thing he envisioned a few years ago, when he planted a few foxgloves in the yard of a Hamptons summer rental. Unlike seeds, you see, one can't always predict how a career will germinate. ■ In the early 1990s, Socia was the art director at *Business Week* magazine. Along with a group of friends, he'd leased a house from the sister of Victoria Fensterer, a legendary gardener best known for her restoration of the landscape surrounding Grey Gardens, the summerhouse of author and editor Ben Bradlee and his wife, society maven Sally Quinn. ■ When Fensterer saw Socia's simple but elegant horticulture, she offered him a part-time job on the spot. "I thought I'd make a few extra

bucks to pay off my AmEx bill, but I fell in love with Victoria's garden," he says with a laugh. "Suddenly I thought, do I really want to spend the rest of my life on the thirty-ninth floor of the McGraw-Hill building, breathing recycled air?" Socia moonlighted with Fensterer for another summer before leaving *Business Week* and Manhattan to live on the East End year-round.

He purchased a former carriage house, built in 1909, located slightly north of East Hampton village. Stucco-clad, its hipped roof and classic proportions charmed Socia. "The place was a wreck, though, and completely overgrown with bittersweet vines," he recalls.

Drawing on a few courses in drafting and architecture he'd taken in college, Socia invested a full year in renovation. While the surrounding landscape took shape, inside the house a dirt-floored entryway blossomed into a cozy salon; the existing kitchen was pruned into a dining room; and the living room flowered into a sleek kitchen. Appropriately

■ 99

Below, right & opposite: In the living room, Persian Heriz rugs enliven the space. A settee from English Country Antiques is covered in Ralph Lauren Home fabric. Navy Donghia mohair covers a chair in the living room. The zebra-striped upholstery is dyed pony skin from Edelman.

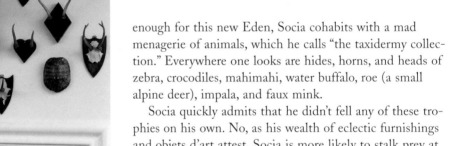

enough for this new Eden, Socia cohabits with a mad menagerie of animals, which he calls "the taxidermy collection." Everywhere one looks are hides, horns, and heads of zebra, crocodiles, mahimahi, water buffalo, roe (a small alpine deer), impala, and faux mink.

Socia quickly admits that he didn't fell any of these trophies on his own. No, as his wealth of eclectic furnishings and objets d'art attest, Socia is more likely to stalk prey at hunting grounds such as the Clignancourt flea market, in Paris. In fact, after the long summer months he spends planning, planting, and — as he often puts it — "fluffing" landscapes in the Hamptons, he travels far afield during the winter months.

Taking such risks in his interior decor seems to steel Socia's nerves for making even bolder leaps in the great outdoors. He tries to instill similar courage in his clients.

"It's peculiar, really. The same person who has no trouble tearing down a wall to double the size of a room can't imagine a tree could be relocated, or removed. This is where I come in," Socia says. "I try to convince them anything's possible, as long as they can tell me what it is they love to look at."

To accomplish such soothsaying, he frequently brings clients to his own yard. Here, a narrow hedgerow pathway leads to an outdoor shower and a shade garden of Elephant

Ear caladiums, hostas, and ostrich ferns. A pair of topiary reindeer gambol in front of a triple-decker hedge made up of privet, yew, and boxwood. By stepping through an antique wrought-iron gate — salvaged from Socia's first apartment in Park Slope, Brooklyn — one sees a hexagonal arbor covered with two types of rose, Eden Climber and New Dawn. Beneath this pink canopy sits whimsically rustic outdoor furniture of Socia's own design, made from Eastern Red Cedar branches.

"This really is my studio," he says, while ruffling the leaves of an enormous boxwood sphere. "As we walk around here together, I make those little circles on my landscape drawings come alive in people's imaginations."

In other words, Craig Socia passes on the exquisite secrets of plant life given to him by his mentor, Victoria Fensterer. The student is now the professor. And so, leaf by leaf, does the garden grow.

Opposite: Given the roaring fireplace, something is always cooking in this kitchen. The sleek, stainless steel cupboards and stools are by Boffi. Above left: The dining room boasts a Tasmanian Blackwood table and Gianni Versace chairs. Above right: An antique portrait keeps watch in the kitchen.

■ 103

TEMPORARY CONTEMPORARY

*On a shoestring budget, Preston Phillips designs a modern
beachside pavilion at Two Mile Hollow.*

"You don't make much of a fee on a one-hundred-fifty-thousand-dollar house," says Preston
Phillips, who, like most architects, works for a percentage. But when Ken Kuchin and Bruce
Anderson, owners of an oceanfront lot in East Hampton, gave the architect that Lilliputian
budget — about what some East End families spend for kitchen cabinets — he was willing.
■ The project brought Phillips, who has been in the Hamptons since 1984, back to his roots,
especially the years he spent working for pioneering modernist architect Paul Rudolph. In
Rudolph's studio, architecture was about experimenting with new ways of using everyday

Opposite & this page: In the living room, designer Shawn Henderson helped the homeowners place furniture, which includes Scandinavian swivel chairs that rotate from view to view.

materials and creating visual complexity from elemental shapes.

The project began when Kuchin and Anderson, who own a gracious home behind a windmill in East Hampton, bought a lot at the end of Two Mile Hollow Road as an investment. But, they figured, why not enjoy the property while they tried to sell it? The two men envisioned a pavilion they would use for weekend getaways — and for parties on a deck overlooking the Atlantic. Besides, the house could help sell the land by showing potential buyers the views from a slight elevation.

But since the men didn't know how long the house would stand — "a new owner may use it as a construction shed," says Kuchin — they didn't want to spend a lot of money. One early plan would have cost $440,000 to build, so they sent Phillips back to the drawing board. Eventually, they settled on a twenty-by-fifty-foot box, raised on stilts and reached by

Opposite & above: A fireplace separates the living room and the bedroom. While the living room side is adorned with a sleek minimal mantel, the bedroom side is inset with shelves to display collections.

■ 107

Below left: Perched on piles anchored in the sand, the house has spectacular views over the double dunes of the Atlantic. An outdoor pavilion attached to the side of the house offers additional entertaining space. Below right: The stair railing made of inexpensive PVC pipes gives graphic directions to the beach. Opposite: The kitchen may look bare-bones, but it's highly functional for this in-town beach house.

a long gangplank with railings made of white PVC tubing. The tubing, in addition to being inexpensive, is strong — each piece can span eight feet, Phillips reports — and maintenance free.

Phillips gave the house a distinctive "butterfly" roof — a shape beloved by early modernists for (literally) inverting the traditional saltbox. For exterior walls, he turned to inexpensive metal barn siding, which is normally seamed vertically; Phillips seamed it horizontally, making a familiar material seem fresh. He chose inexpensive, aluminum-framed windows but used them in twos or threes to maximize the vistas.

Interior walls are straight out of Home Depot — plywood trimmed with cedar and treated with clear stain. To keep the open feeling, Phillips eschewed partitions (a two-sided fireplace separates the living from the bedroom area). The ceiling, painted azure blue, creates the illusion that the sky flows through the building. Indeed, wherever possible, the architect let nature prevail over architecture. Yet the effect is hardly unsophisticated.

Getting the house built wasn't easy. "When you have one

108 ◾

Left & above: A Papa Bear chair from Antik has wood paws on the armrests that complement the designs of Anthony Brozna, a furniture maker. Brozna, whose style is influenced by Japanese and Scandinavian forms, created more than a dozen pieces for the house, including a desk that folds out from the wall and a bed with floating side tables.

bathroom, how are you going to get the plumber to come out?" Phillips asks. "He's doing houses with twelve bathrooms." But even before it was complete, the house attracted attention. Some neighbors found it flashy and out of place. Others admired it for recalling the days when East Enders thought more about the stars above than the stars at Nick and Toni's.

Of course, the house doesn't exactly portend a new asceticism, given that its owners use it as a retreat from a much larger retreat. But, however the house is used, it is architecturally significant as a reminder that simple buildings can be stirring. Phillips may not have made a lot of money, but he made his point.

Rooms with a View

Landscape architect Perry Guillot envisions new gardens, while Arthur Dunnam re-dresses the interiors of a historic Victorian Italianate villa in Sag Harbor.

Historic houses come with rich histories, but they also present the classic preservation conflict between restoration and renovation. While a strict period restoration may save a significant image of the past, it's rarely very livable. A sensitive renovation, on the other hand, can enhance the vitality of a home. ■ In the 1860s, Hannibal French, a whaling captain, transformed a modest house built in 1799 into a grand Victorian Italianate villa. Built on Main Street in Sag Harbor, this stretch became known as Captains' Row because of the many whaling captains' homes that lined it. A symbol of the wealth that once flooded Sag Harbor from ports near and far, the French house is one of the largest private

*Opposite & this page: In the architecture
and on the grounds, a fleur-de-lis design
is seen in two media. Bold, sculptural
shapes define the garden.*

residences in the village and features extraordinary detail along with a beautiful sense of scale.

When the current owners decided to rework the interiors and gardens, they called upon two experts who would respect the original architecture without being limited by it. Despite the home's air of sophistication, the owners wanted an atmosphere that would be decidedly unfussy — a second home that would give a nod to the past but still fill their need for a respite from Manhattan.

Perry Guillot, a Southampton-based landscape architect, was called on to reimagine the grounds that wrap the house. Inextricably linked to the powerful nineteenth-century architecture, Guillot recognized that the gardens and interiors needed to function in concert with each other. His design maintains a continual, yet subtle, conversation between house and garden. Interior windows with ornate molding frame the

Above: A perfectly oval pool, located on a center axis with the house, is a bright blue gem in the center of the lush green garden. Opposite: Ornate molding surrounds a dining room window and frames a garden view.

114 ■

Opposite: Antique wicker sofa and chairs from the American Wing lend a casual feel to the breakfast room. The nineteenth-century Dutch brass chandelier is from Sag Harbor Antiques, and the vintage pillow fabric is from a Jean Sinenberg antiques show. Below left: Blue shutters adorn the Victorian Italianate villa on Sag Harbor's Captains' Row. Below right: Designer Arthur Dunnam created a number of custom pieces for this project, including the dining room table and replicas of eighteenth-century Swedish neoclassical dining chairs. The raffia and string carpet is from Beauvais.

views. Using only three plant species — American boxwood, white Iceberg roses, and common privet — Guillot created formal, yet minimal, French-style gardens. While the look might seem at odds with a whaling captain's house, "the house demanded a formal garden, and that is what was appropriate," he explains.

It is a garden whose symmetrical plan also complements the exterior architecture. A boxwood-bordered rose parterre sits behind the former ballroom. It is an elegant statement with a fleur-de-lis design taken from the house's frieze. Because symmetry is paramount to Guillot, the oval pool was placed on a central axis to the house, as well as to the rose parterre and patio.

Using privet was somewhat daring. Guillot did so only in the back garden and kept it to a low five feet, which allowed unbroken views to the nearby Whaling Museum and Customs House — each a landmark. "Sag Harbor is about gorgeous, low-scaled fences," Guillot explains. "They are part of the neighborly character and mood of the historic village." Privet shouldn't be used here in the same way it is in other South Fork villages, he believes, so Guillot framed the rear garden with embracing hedges in a large oval shape that echoes the pool.

Even though the garden plan is formal, its edges are softened and rounded by the wide arc of hedge. "The size of the elements introduced into the garden plan are simple and

■ 117

Right: Dunnam developed an elegant living room decorative scheme by dressing formal gilt metal side chairs in a playful Fonthill check. The Klismos-style table is from R. E. Steele Antiques.

large, which keeps the whole composition in scale with this mighty house," Guillot says.

For the interiors, the owners turned to Arthur Dunnam of Jed Johnson Associates to reinvigorate the architecture. "My clients loved the historic flourishes of the house, so we just let them be. We didn't want to homogenize the house and remove the character by taking away its authentic quirkiness," Dunnam says.

Ease and sophistication were achieved in the former ball-room-cum-living room with eighteenth-century Swedish furnishings. For a bit of flair and a nod to the twentieth century, Art Deco pieces were added to the mix. Many pieces of the furniture were treated with milk paint to give them a chalky, aged patina. Painted by local decorative painters Chris Butler and Paul Sterzek, the pieces look as though they were always at home here.

Working with the beauty of this historic home, Dunnam and Guillot let it be the springboard—not the dictator—for their aesthetic choices. They let what already existed guide them in creating a home that honors the past while living for today.

BLOCKBUSTER

A Manhattan architect reimagines a second-generation contemporary into a weekend retreat that renews the spirit of modern living on the East End.

The modernist architectural movement left a number of significant structures dotting the East End landscape. But the movement also spawned countless less-pedigreed siblings: the cube- and shoebox-shaped houses that abound from the dunes of Westhampton to the Northwest Woods of East Hampton. These contemporary, geometric houses proliferated from the 1960s well into the 1980s, promising the crest of Manhattan's baby boom a modern weekend lifestyle in "the country." ■ Ed Krug and John Haubrich found their retreat from the city in a neglected "builder special" in East Hampton. Krug, the director of a creative services company in Manhattan, had lived in California for six years and was looking for a weekend house that reflected a more modern sensibility — an East Coast version of

the lifestyle that he experienced on the West Coast.

The house Krug and Haubrich bought in 1996 was built by a local developer for his family about 1969. After about ten years, it eventually became a rental property and entered a long period of neglect and decline.

"For twenty-five years people had just put in and left things in the yard," says Haubrich, a graphic designer and artist. "The backyard was absolute woods with trees all the way up to the deck." The original house consisted of a main vertical box with the living room and guestroom below and the master bedroom above. An enclosed breezeway housed the dining room and kitchen and connected a smaller square box, which is now a study.

Krug and Haubrich turned to a friend, Manhattan-based architect Stephen Alton, to help them renovate and expand the house with a painting studio for Haubrich, plus a carport. While they all recognized the house as a somewhat

■ 123

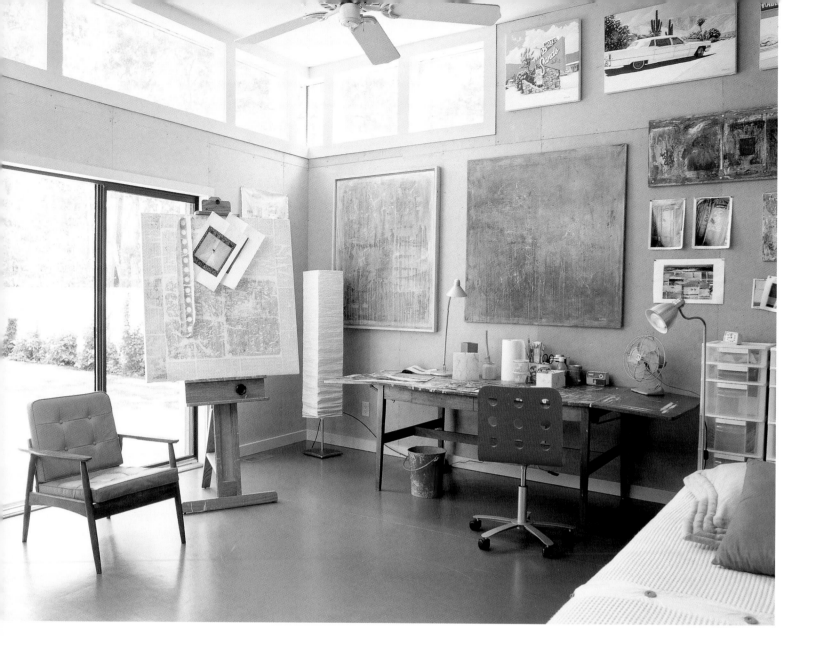

typical "contemporary," the property clearly needed develop-
ment with a site plan. "On a formal level, we were trying to
recognize the architecture that was there and add balance,"
says Alton. "We were trying to give the house better proportions by adding a third volume to the right."

Alton and his clients decided to refresh the house through
the choice of exterior materials. "We were not necessarily
interested in copying what was already there, but we didn't
want to ignore what the building was. I was interested in the
layering of the building and expressing that on the surfaces,"
Alton adds. Settling on Laticrete, a standard fiber/cement
board used to clad buildings, Alton made a key decision to
leave its surface uncoated. "We left it exposed as the outer
surface," Alton says. "It's actually the protective surface in
building that is typically covered with stucco."

While the clients loved the dark gray color of the Laticrete, as well as the exposed screw heads that held the panels

*Above: In the studio addition, Alton maximizes light with a strip
of eyebrow windows. The floor is covered in an artist-friendly
material called Lonseal, which is easy to clean. Opposite: A detail
from the exterior of the studio shows the eyebrow windows floating
above the cedar lattice.*

124 ∎

in place, neighbors were at first startled and concerned about the aesthetic direction of the house. Taking inspiration from the vertical cypress board and batten on the main box of the house, Alton's plan also called for a layer of vertical cedar lattice installed as a wrap around the studio and carport. "I like the play of transparency with the lattice," Alton explains. The natural brown finish of the wood gives the gray Laticrete a warmth and texture. Along the side of the carport, where there is no Laticrete, the lattice offers an airy semiprivacy from the neighbors — and vice versa.

The result of Alton's addition and architectural update is a house that appears more twenty-first-century contemporary than late-sixties builder special. "Sometimes things feel like they're exactly what they're supposed to be," Krug says.

"One of the things that we really love about the house is that it's close to the center of town but very quiet where we live," Haubrich adds. "There's a wonderful sense of being separated from the village in our own environment. We love all the glass and the fact that you're inside but outside all year round."

Opposite: For a headboard, Krug and Haubrich use a Japanese lacquered screen from Apsara. Above: The original board-and-batten surface provided inspiration for Alton's vertical cedar lattice that wraps the carport and studio addition.

In the Country

"Hamptons Story" by Rona Jaffe

The story of my happy union with the Hamptons began as many marriages do: numerous unsatisfactory dates with others, a meeting where you think at least this one is better, or, perhaps, fall in love at first sight, and then the surprise — even if overdue — commitment.

I started renting here when I was in my twenties, in a share in East Hampton. It was a hovel. At night I gave cocktail parties, inviting the men I had met on the beach that day, and a few girls. But I disliked the house and disliked my share partners more, and when in August I got the opportunity to go to Italy to write a magazine article, I happily accepted the chance to escape.

I didn't rent again in the Hamptons for many years. Then, after a fifteen-year relationship with the man I thought I would spend my old age with ended sadly and too soon, on the advice of friends I rented a house in the Hamptons again, this time in Wainscott, this time by myself. I liked the house, and invited guests all summer long, but it never occurred to me to live there permanently.

A few summers later, I tried a blind date with Sagaponack. Right away I was enchanted by the fields, the silvery quality of the light that has attracted artists to the Hamptons for many years, and the roughness of the meadow in front of the house. The owner let me stay there for six months instead of just the summer. This gave me a chance to see what other seasons were like on the East End.

Meanwhile I could see the house next door from my window. It was big and looked like a child's drawing of a house. It was nothing experimental or modern or odd: just a farmhouse. I knew it would be for rent the next summer. I went to see the nicely decorated inside twice. Both times I kept thinking: This house is too good for me. It's too good for my messy guests, with their undisciplined dogs, their wild children. It's too big, too grownup. It's a commitment. I'd have to be brave. But I was infatuated.

Then the owners decided they didn't want to rent, they wanted to sell. Suddenly my love object was about to be lost. If you don't marry me I'm leaving.

Unexpectedly, another suitor appeared for my house. This wall-flower, which had languished on the market for two years, was suddenly the object of a price war. Within a week I had gotten a loan and committed to buy the house for cash: so I won. I even managed to buy all the furniture, which was exactly to my taste.

I was in shock.

I've lived there for almost eight years. I've written parts of several novels there. I have made many wonderful friends in the Hamptons. But for years, every week something else in my house broke. It was like the difficult early days of a marriage between strangers when they discover faults in each other: passionate, angry, fighting and making up.

Dealing with my house is a little easier now. Things don't break so often, and when they do I'm more sanguine about it. I realize it's how you build a relationship. You fix things, you forgive, you move on together. You plant flowers and look at them from your porch, glad to be there, surprised it's lasted so long, hoping it will last longer. That's my Hamptons story.

Rona Jaffe is a novelist. She lives in Sagaponack and New York City.

LA BELLA CASA

Designer Ted Tyler creates a backwoods Italian cottage in Springs that's a testament to the delights of deliberation.

Do you want a Hamptons house in a hurry? Then read no further. For if you dream of a pop-up palace surrounded by sod rolled out like wrapping paper, the tale of Ted Tyler will hold no appeal for you. His weekend cottage is testament to the delights of deliberation. ■ A well-respected designer of handmade fabrics and wall coverings, Tyler spent weekends in East Hampton village for many years. Gradually hemmed in by crowds and noise, he began searching for a more tranquil spot. He finally found one in Springs, alongside Accabonac Harbor. ■ The first four years he owned the property, Tyler did nothing but tramp through underbrush, clearing vines and weeds, identifying trees, and learning as much as he could of the patterns of light, wind, and sky as the seasons changed. "People out

Opposite: The house as seen from the box-wood garden. This page: The living room features TylerGraphic fabrics, including Rose Du Roi on the sofa and Big Basket and Peony on the floor pillows.

here tend to buy, bulldoze, and then spend fortunes to put trees back in," he says. "My goal was to save as much as I could of what was already here."

Inspired by a dreamy, sepia-toned photograph of an unfinished house in Renaissance Italy designed by Andrea Palladio, Tyler became enchanted by the romantic notion of a stone tower. He imagined a masonry structure that would appear abandoned in the woods — and only at some later date rediscovered and added to with two structural wings built of wood.

Collaborating with Jeff Hagedon, a friend and an interior designer, Tyler spent many months sketching. He fully embraced the quirks of working organically, not imposing rules, but allowing the site to dictate the house's scale and flow. In fact, this process was quite similar to the way he designs a fabric or wall-covering pattern. Tyler is an unabashed Luddite and adheres to old-fashioned methods of pen and ink and cut and paste rather than a computer-generated click and drag.

Opposite: A formal boxwood garden sits nestled between the two "spokes" of the house. The fir doors of the living room open into the garden. Above: The guest bedroom is in the other spoke and also borders the garden. The TylerGraphic fabric on the near bed is Big Basket. The far bed is clad in Peony fabric with a pillow in Big Top.

■ 135

Below: Oars grace the entry hall-way of the house. The wall covering is Text by TylerGraphic.

Right: An interior stone wall, fashioned as though once part of the exterior, sports a plastic cow's head from a Winn-Dixie supermarket. Opposite: Designer Ted Tyler fell in love with the idea of a stone tower. The tower forms the core of the house, which also has two wings, or "spokes," radiating out from it. Tyler built the wherry (a rowing shell) from a kit. He takes it out for voyages around Accabonac Harbor.

"I strive to have the hand shown in my fabrics," he says. "It's almost an Arts and Crafts sensibility, and I wanted that same feel for this house."

The dwelling is essentially composed of four large rooms: a living room, a combined kitchen and dining room, a guestroom with an adjoining bath, and a master suite. Its cedar-shake facades blend harmoniously into the landscape, most of which Tyler has left to grow wild. All window casements and doors are painted what he calls "Frank Lloyd Wright Cherokee red."

Intentionally or not, there is something distinctly Wrightian, too, in how the outside and inside merge through a profusion of mullioned glass doors and carefully framed views. Since the rooms are "spokes" from the stone tower, all have exposures on three sides. Built into the tower's second floor, Tyler's bedroom (with a cozy balcony) is almost like a tree house. Its windows face a view of sun-dappled oaks and, off in the distance, the brilliant chartreuse of a salt marsh.

"One thing you learn from designing textiles is balance," Tyler says. "You don't want there to be 'hot spots' in the design, meaning places that draw undue focus."

Consequently, throughout Tyler's house little visual clutter occurs. By and large, walls are empty, tabletops are left clear, and the fireplace has no mantel on which decorative objects might collect. A few "homage to Warhol" sculptures done by

Tyler when he was a student at San Francisco Art Institute in the late 1970s can be found, but mostly his choice of natural materials is decor enough.

As the prevailing calm is disturbed only occasionally by the chirp of an osprey flying overhead, Tyler admits he sometimes doesn't leave his property all weekend. He might go sculling on a wooden boat called a wherry that he built by hand last winter. More often than not, though, he sits drawing at an enormous cherry table in the living room, mixing business with pleasure. "I get more work done out here than I do in the city," he says, with an almost guilty smile.

Opposite: In the core tower of the house, the kitchen can be found down a step from the living area. The cabinetry and tables were custom made for the house. The near table, made of walnut, is dressed in TylerGraphic Monkey Business fabric. The curtains are in the TylerGraphic pattern Pears. Above: In the tower above the kitchen, the master bedroom enjoys a high perch.

■ 139

Opposite: What now serves as the downstairs guest bedroom would have been used as a parlor in the eighteenth century. When Gardiner purchased the house, the windows in the room were made up of a six-over-six pane arrangement common in the 1800s. She had the original twelve-over-twelve layout — like the house, a relic of the 1700s — duplicated and restored. The beds are eighteenth-century rope beds, which may give guests a real feeling of age. Below left: Guests can enjoy one of the home's three fireplaces. Below right: Above the mantel, a world map traces the route of the Dawn *on its whaling voyages. Unlike many artifacts in the house, the map is a modern-day re-creation, not an authentic piece.*

New York City in the 1820s on *Pequod*-like journeys around the Horn to the Pacific. More than a hundred years later, during Pi's youth, the Gardiner house teemed with whaling relics — the captain's log, scrimshaw, and other souvenirs Captain Gardiner had gathered in his forays around the South Sea Islands.

Many of the relics have since been donated to the Cold Springs Harbor Whaling Museum, but the spirit of whaling and the past infuses Pi Gardiner's persona and her home. A traditional center-chimney, Long Island home from the mid-eighteenth century, it sits on the Gardiner family land near the Quogue Canal. But it didn't always — and therein lies the third family history, to which Gardiner can now lay claim.

"When it was time for my own place, my husband and I wanted to buy an old home," Gardiner says. On the North Fork, in Cutchogue, they found the home of their dreams — a 1750 shingled home in reasonable condition. "It was all original — covers, doors, latches, and all of the detailing that could easily have been ripped out," she recalls. Perhaps as importantly, the home's history did not end with its fixtures.

■ 143

"The same family, the Hortons, had lived there forever. It was a remarkable story that reminded me of my own family's history."

The fact that the home they'd discovered sat far from their family land on the South Fork did not deter Gardiner and her husband. They bought the home, took it apart in four pieces, and moved it on a flatbed truck to Quogue, where it was reassembled. "In the old days, we would have moved it by boat," she says wistfully.

Working with Eastport-based craftsman Nathan Tuttle, who helped restore the Halsey homestead in Southampton, Gardiner endeavored to reconstruct the home to its current

state. Small touches, like the worn wooden shelves in the "buttery," were carefully preserved. The kitchen, modernized before the Gardiners' purchase, kept to the historic tone with eighteenth-century slate counters and floors.

Additions to the original structure, probably made in the early 1800s, house the study, kitchen, and downstairs guest bedroom. Upstairs, a loft has been converted into three bedrooms and two bathrooms.

Gardiner's love for old houses and American furniture extends beyond her home to her job as the executive director of the Merchant's House Museum on East Fourth Street in Manhattan. "I was working in corporate strategic planning,

and a colleague asked if I'd ever been to the old Merchant's House. I'd never heard of it," Gardiner recalls. "I stumbled on it and drop-dead fell in love with it. Next thing I knew, I was the director."

Working out of the Merchant's House, an 1832 brick row house, Gardiner has also overseen the creation of the New York Oyster Festival, which brings forty thousand people to the streets of Manhattan each October. Every June, Gardiner and the museum host a garden-party benefit; in 2004 the theme was Greek Revival. Throughout it all, Gardiner's passion for preservation shines through. "Bridgehampton really was potato fields," she adds. "We'd better wake up, because when it's gone, it's gone."

Above: Much of the wood furniture found throughout the house has been in Gardiner's family for generations. Opposite: A view of the dining room table, another antique piece.

IN THE EYE
OF THE BEHOLDER

*A house becomes a home when a connoisseur finds an
architectural gem hiding in the woods.*

In the early 1990s, Anita Calero, a Manhattan-based photographer, drove out to the East End
looking for something "small and studio loft–like." After years of weekends in upstate New
York, she had finally determined to find her place in the Hamptons. ■ Buried in the woods
on the border between East Hampton and the Springs, she found an architectural gem. In
the early sixties, Richard Bender, an architect, had built a moderately priced, modernist
weekend house for himself. Then, as now, staking a real-estate claim in the Hamptons took
some creative planning. Bender purchased, with a group of associates, a twenty-acre parcel
of land in the woods and subdivided it into smaller lots for each party. He then built his

Opposite: A glimpse of Anita Calero's design sensibility. This page: Window walls line two sides of the house. Steps lead down to the garden, where Calero and her friend Miguel Pons installed boulders to anchor views from the house.

house as a model for the others to follow. This progressive subdivision was called Amenity.

Alastair Gordon explores the vibrant history of modern living in the Hamptons in his book *Weekend Utopia*. "The Amenity houses were designed using a modular system, standard building parts, and prefabricated framing to save costs. The 850-square foot houses had small sun decks, Japanese-style landscaping, and cost less than $15,000 to build (including furniture and landscaping but without central heating)," Gordon writes.

Wrapped on two sides by walls of glass, the house still evoked the spirit of indoor/outdoor living when Calero found it. Time and the weather, though, had not been so kind to the "affordable" materials with which it was built. "I redid it over again but with new materials," Calero says. While the original Formica-fronted cabinets were in good enough shape to keep in place, the plywood on the half wall separating the kitchen and the living area was replaced with a more-finished-looking ash plywood. All of the sliding doors and pine floors were replaced.

■ 151

"It had been a purely summerhouse," Calero says. "The outside shower was just a hose. And there was no heat." Still using the house primarily in the summer, Calero thrives on the beauty of nature just outside her walls of windows. "The house is like a big leaf under so many trees, and I live under that leaf," Calero emphasizes in her soft Spanish-inflected English.

The gardens were nonexistent until Calero started respectfully improving the surrounding grounds. Miguel Pons, a friend and landscape designer, brought in specimen rocks from as far away as Connecticut. Carefully selected, they act as focal points against the surrounding forest. Every room now has some view of a large boulder outside. Calero speaks of them reverentially. "The big one is the heart of the house," she adds. Before launching a career in photography, Calero

Above: Indigo is the color of choice for the master bedroom. The quilt is a patchwork of kimonos from the 1800s. The indigo panel of fabric above the bed is from Cora Ginsburg and hangs from a vintage shoulder-carrying pole, from Youngblood Gallery. Opposite: Decks extend the house's living area in summer.

152 ■

Opposite: Calero's dining table was originally a cafeteria table designed by Eames. Russell Wright designed the chairs. Below left: Backyard landscaping echoes the house's design scheme. Below right: Calero found a 1920s Japanese door in a gallery on Madison Avenue in Manhattan. Captivated by its surface, she gave it a new life as a bed headboard in the guest bedroom. A demure Mexican statuette was made into a lamp. A cow skin from her father in Colombia is layered on a wool rug from ABC Carpet and Home.

was very successful as a stylist of home furnishings, fashion, and jewelry. Like the still lifes she's become known for styling and photographing, Calero has thoughtfully composed (she would never call it decorating) her home.

In the master and guest bedrooms, panels of fabrics hang above or beside the beds. It's a celebration of subtle texture and the heady elegance of simplicity. "Joe D'Urso is a big influence on me," Calero says. D'Urso is a designer whose career was launched with the high-tech/high-touch movement in the seventies.

In many ways, one could say that this house was actually built for Calero, who came to the Hamptons looking for a home that would reconnect her to the beauty and simplicity of nature. Fortunately, this ambitious little house was found and restored by a kindred spirit.

■ 155

AMERICAN ANTHEM

In Wainscott's disappearing rural landscape, Robert Stilin found temporary haven in a renovated New England barn.

Few architectural structures reflect the American spirit the way a barn does. Cathedral-like interiors offer wide-open living spaces, while no-nonsense, rough-hewn beams and wide plank floors add a hearty grace to their design. Although the East End has its own distinctive potato barns, a number of other barn styles — from metal-clad "sheds" to boxy New England structures — can be found scattered across the county's remaining fields. ■ Robert Stilin, an East Hampton–based interior designer, found temporary quarters — between selling a house and building a new one — in a Wainscott barn relocated from New England. The barn's previous owner had converted the barn into a house in part by enhancing the two-storied living room with towering multipane windows that flood it

Opposite: The American flag hangs from the rafters. This page: A sampling from Stilin's collection of chairs fills the double-height living room. Ray LeClaire fashioned tight slipcovers in Henry Calvin's Rex Linen for the sofa and club chairs.

Below left: The gentle light of the East End floods through the tall windows, working its magic in the living room. Stilin uses an antique copper weather vane as sculpture on the sofa table. Below right & opposite: An eclectic collection of chairs lines a wall.

with light. The loft-like spaces easily accommodated Stilin's furniture.

The project offered a clean canvas to this self-taught decorator. "I fell into interior design completely by accident," Stilin explains. After a bad experience with an interior designer who had been hired to renovate an earlier home of his in Palm Beach, "I just decided I could do it better myself," he says. In Palm Beach, Stilin owned a home furnishings shop on Via Pariggi, which quickly evolved into interior design work for friends and, later, collaborative projects with Los Angeles–based interior designer Waldo. By 1995 Stilin was spending

Above: In a sitting room under the loft, shelves filled with books surround a window. A weathered Arts and Crafts table holds an arrangement of natural and antique objects. Opposite: A room created in the loft makes a snug master bedroom under the rafters.

Opposite: A round table makes for easy, friendly dinners. The mix of chairs gathered around the table is like a group of good friends with a variety of personalities and styles. Left: The low-beamed ceiling creates an inviting room for watching movies. A dark brown Nancy Corzine chenille covers the sofa. The large, plump pillows in a fabric from Rogers & Goffigon Ltd. invite relaxation. A cut-down farm table serves as a cocktail table. Below: Enlivening a cozy corner are a check fabric from Chelsea Editions and a striped fabric from Ian Mankin.

more than half of each year in East Hampton, and in 2000, he moved with his son to the East End full time.

He admits to having had reservations about living — even temporarily — in a former barn. "I reused things from previous houses and simply made it all work," he says matter-of-factly. Inspired by Robert Wilson's chair collection at the Watermill Center, Stilin filled the rooms with chairs from his own collection, giving the barn a revival air.

"I also collect American flags. I love the crispness and patina of the material. And, they're a wonderful alternative to other kinds of art," Stilin says. "Although things changed a little after September 11, I still find them all the time, and I've never paid more than three hundred to four hundred dollars for one." The attraction is no anomaly. "I like things that are aged," he adds. "If I had a choice, I'd rather have something old than something new."

THE ART OF LIVING

Arnie Lizan and Elizabeth Tops live with exuberant style in their colorful home deep in the Northwest Woods.

Chartreuse. Not the liqueur invented by Carthusian monks, but an acid shade of green that's half lemon, half lime. This color pops up frequently in the vibrantly decorated house of art dealers Arnie Lizan and Elizabeth Tops. Truth to tell, so do purple, hot pink, orange, and turquoise. Yet, it's the chartreuse — on pillows, chairs, even tableware — that most confounds. ■ "It's the natural color of spring," Lizan suggests, "but bumped up a notch." Unsatisfied with this explanation, Tops quotes from a poem by Dylan Thomas: "The force that through the green fuse drives the flower, drives my green age." Her grin is that of a born show-off, but a student's diligence furrows her forehead. ■ A similar tension — between ostentation and erudition — sparks the couple's weekend house in East Hampton's

Opposite: Arnie Lizan and Elizabeth Tops's house is tucked discreetly into the Northwest Woods of East Hampton. However, the overscaled bust of Archimedes by Alex Giannis makes a bold statement heralding the house's art-filled interiors. This page: Chartreuse and purple fabrics up the ante in this sitting area. Lizan found the checkered chairs, which are English theater seats, at Takashimaya, in New York City, where they were used as display props. Decorator Noel Jeffrey chose a customized circular carpet by Edward Fields to anchor the furniture.

Opposite: A tall bronze figure by Gary Weissman attracts attention in the living room. On the recamier, Jeffrey opted for a solid black fabric over a more expected velvet or damask. Gold nails heighten the look. Left: A flower-filled stone urn from Canyan Antiques is the centerpiece of a dining table set with Christian Dior's leopard and palm trees china. Below: Colorful, handblown glasses by Charles Provenzano look their best in a light-filled room.

Northwest Woods. Its traditional white-clapboard exterior gives little hint of the visual pyrotechnics inside, where antiques and modern furniture are juxtaposed almost recklessly. There's also a dazzling collection of paintings and sculpture, much of it by artists who showed at the couple's Lizan Tops Gallery on Newtown Lane, in East Hampton. The house is equal parts museum and thrill ride — all covered with a big dollop of "look ma, no hands!"

It was not always thus. When Lizan and Tops first drove up six years ago, they encountered a drab, three-bedroom cottage built in the 1980s, with plaster mushrooms dotting the front lawn. The site, however — a sunny hill surrounded by trees and only a quarter mile from Northwest Harbor — showed promise. They immediately hired architect Aryeh Siegel, who completely reconfigured the original structure and added two wings: a large living room at one end and a guest bedroom suite plus porte cochere on the other.

Exactly as Lizan and Tops advise their clients, plans for interior design began with a complete assessment of their art portfolio. Aided by their decorator, Noel Jeffrey, and before any furniture was arranged, the couple placed canvases by Henri Matisse, Milton Avery, Connie Fox, and Dan Rizzie.

"We are educators, not just salespeople," Lizan says. "Someone will have all this after us. We are just cataloging it for future generations."

Below left: The elegant black glass vases on a shelf in the living room were designed by artist Dante Marioni. Below right & opposite: Between two colorful bright chairs stands a nineteenth-century French Empire table detailed with an eagle crest. The white finish and white marble top is an interesting variation from the traditional mahogany of that period. The signature chartreuse on the Bridgewater chair is Valognes by Manuel Canovas. Above the mosaic-trimmed fireplace is a 1940s Venetian mirror from Palm Beach; the silver-leaf lamp is also from the 1940s. The sisal rug is from Patterson, Flynn & Martin.

He isn't speaking metaphorically, either, as reference manuals, encyclopedias, art catalogs, and books about artists are stacked everywhere. Curious about those Etruscan engravings or that abstract tapestry by the little-known Dutch weaver Jan Yoors? Simply ask the question, and Lizan or Tops will generously find a text (perhaps several) that offers further information. Admittedly, not all of their belongings are to everyone's taste. "Bronx Nouveau" is how Tops's mother derides a pair of squat, eighteenth-century Italian armchairs reupholstered in tufted turquoise silk. Yet, everything has a story.

At least until the "professors" retire and head to a master suite decorated solely in (aaaaahhh!) white. This bedroom is an oasis from the public areas' colorful exuberance.

"When you go to bed, you want peace," Tops says. She then laughs as she admits, "Guests are even afraid to go in to our room. They think they'll get it dirty." Guests at lunch or dinner, that is, not for the weekend. Although the couple nearly tripled their house's size with the renovation, they still managed to lose a bedroom. "We built this place for us. Not for resale, and not for guests," Tops explains. "Arnie always

168 ■

Opposite: In stark contrast to the other rooms in the house, the master bedroom is a pristine white. Bergamo sheers dress the bed. Below: The guest bedroom is "an ode to Hollywood in the fifties," says decorator Jeffrey. The headboard is vintage, and the custom bedspread with black rosettes was designed in white fabric from Brunschwig & Fils. A canvas by Alex Giannis hangs above a Lewis Mittman sofa. The shag rug is by Patterson, Flynn & Martin.

tells people they can stay as late as they like, they can even come back for breakfast, but they go to their own bed to sleep."

Instead of being inhospitable, they may simply be guarding themselves against how easily people fall under the spell of this house. "We bought it for ourselves, for this exact spot, yet we have clients who are obsessed. . . ." His voice trails off, reflecting on the situation.

"We may have to part with it," Tops agrees. Expecting no pity, they both shrug. Having built a house that's a frame for art, they know full well who created this predicament.

■ 171

PLAY HOUSE

*Call the Shelter Island house of Jonathan Adler and Simon Doonan
what you will, but it's anything but dull.*

"Playfulness has become antithetical to art. It's sad that only dour people seem to be taken seriously." This lament is offered by Jonathan Adler, who refers to himself as a "Joni Mitchell–lovin', Birkenstock-wearin', dream-weavin' potter." He makes these remarks while sitting in the living room of the Shelter Island weekend house he owns with Simon Doonan, a *New York Observer* columnist and creative director of Barney's. ■ The couple fell in love with Shelter Island in the mid-1990s after renting a house one summer near Sunset Beach. While biking around the island looking for a "little modernist cracker box," they finally saw an asymmetrical A-frame "shack" just a few yards from Crab Creek. Its provenance seemed almost too good to be true. "We were told it was built by a Pan Am pilot in the sixties,"

Opposite: The exterior of the house, with water transportation. This page: Punchy sixties chairs by Pierre Paulin, a custom Victoriana scalloped rug, and pillows by Adler — plus Doonan's book Wacky Chicks — *complete the tangy color scheme of the loft.*

Opposite: The living room as seen from the loft. Here, rugs, pottery, pillows, and a lamp — all designed by Adler — share an open living space with a Richard Schultz petal table and a large John-Paul Philippe painting. The canvas bag is from the nearby Boltax Gallery. White walls throughout let the furnishings and accessories command the attention. Above left: A wood-burning stove is part of the entranceway. Above right: A guestroom is perched above the living room behind the beaded curtains. Adler created a bedspread with the word "guest" woven in a seventies digital font. The sconces are from a Palm Beach thrift shop.

says Doonan. "We immediately pulled out the checkbook."

Adler notes that subsequent renovations added "a bit of Santa Fe and a bit of country cottage" to the three-bedroom and two-bath house, but this was rectified by "a lick of white paint." This provides a blank backdrop for the couple's ever-changing arrangement of art, much of which is made by friends or family members. This trove includes everything from tin figures of Don Quixote and plaster garden gnomes to a needlepoint of Miss Piggy and a Plexiglas portrait of Japan's Princess Masako. As long as all the colors are strong, the men believe that nothing clashes. They may be right; the overall effect — to borrow a phrase from Doonan's hilarious book, *Wacky Chicks* — is "stark, raving mod."

■ 175

Below left: The light-filled master bedroom shows Adler's wood-gourd lamp at bedside. The wall hanging was bought on a trip through the mountains of Peru. Below right: A sixties lightbulb lamp by Ingo Maurer salvaged from Adler's parents' attic hangs over a local yard-sale find, a vintage Paul Evans table. The "Coloniana" chairs were found on Shelter Island at Marika's and painted red. The pots are from Adler's Capuchine collection. Opposite: In their element at the studio: Adler at the wheel, Doonan on the phone, and Liberace meditating.

"Minimalism is a bummer," Adler adds. "It's very varied around here. You might even say it's schizophrenic."

Some stylistic sanity is provided by pieces from the Jonathan Adler Collection. His sinuous lamps, vases, and slipcast figures — of a hippopotamus, for example, or a blowfish — are mostly made in Lima, Peru. During multiple trips there, Adler forged relationships with local artisans, who now weave a variety of alpaca wool pillows, throws, and rugs for him. These, which he calls "Marimekko meets Machu Picchu," are decorated in bold geometrics or with fanciful shapes such as hearts or butterflies. "You might say we live in a fully-branded household," Adler says, sweeping his arm forth in a supreme gesture of self-mocking grandeur.

176 ■

Opposite: The loft office features a Fornasetti chair, vintage campaign-style desk refurbished in purple, and vintage keys as wall ornaments. The platinum lamp, lacquer box, and vase are by Adler. Left: A cozy guest bedroom is filled with Adler accessories plus another John-Paul Philippe painting and vintage George Nelson end tables. Below: A painting by Adler's father rests near an African chair and vintage dresser.

"Yes, but living with your things informs their design," Doonan interjects. "I'm always dubious of fashion designers who don't wear their own clothes. What does that say?"

"Good point, little stuff," Adler replies, as Doonan returns to his desk, on top of which perches a statuette of Napoléon.

Assuming France's "little corporal" offers him inspiration, it's rather surprising how nonimperial, even hands-off, Doonan has been with this cottage's appearance. After years of overseeing display at one of America's premier emporiums — not to mention issuing design diktat each week in "Simon Says," his *New York Observer* column — one might guess that Doonan would have an opinion or two at home. "I may be the bossy boots at Barney's, but around here, my suggestions are met with a curl of Johnny's lip," he says. "I get such a chuckle out of it. I'll be here reading, and Johnny comes charging through the door with some insane Victorian doodad. I look up and say, 'That's wonderful, honey.' He takes it to the garage and paints it cerise."

Not quite sure what cerise looks like? Think pink, like the floor of the small loft bedroom upstairs, which overlooks the living room. Here is a Fornasetti chair, a campaign desk (painted purple), a grotesquely large ceramic snail, and yes, an insane Victorian doodad that acts as a bookshelf. Adler looks it all over with a contented smile. "Not to sound too Pollyanna-ish, but the spirit of this house is sincere," he concludes. "We've had some of our happiest times here."

Camp Baratta

*Nautical themes meet the Wild West in an updated summer boys'
camp–styled house that Anthony Baratta has created in Flanders.*

Oh? You don't know about Flanders? And you say you know the Hamptons? Well, okay,
you're not alone. The discovery of a virtually unknown hamlet in these parts gives one hope
that the "old Hamptons" still exists somewhere — and it promises freedom from the traffic
stranglehold of Route 27. Indeed, both features have kept Anthony Baratta, of the Manhattan-
based decorating firm Diamond Baratta Design, coming to his Flanders home for more
than twenty years. ■ "I used to work for a husband-and-wife art director team many years
ago, and I bought the house from them," recalls Baratta. "This neighborhood was like the
end of the earth. Just a few houses for weekend fishermen, and then on the other side, it
was all locals. But we ended up forming a very tight community." ■ The 1952 house, in a

Opposite: A lighthouse painting hangs against a collection of National Geographic *magazines. This page: Old Glory shines on the screened porch.*

woodsy spot just feet from Flanders Bay, retains much of its vintage charm. Walls and vaulted ceilings are whitewashed wood, and the original kitchen is casually laid out along a wall of the long living room. "The man who owned this way back had all the walls made of unpainted knotty pine. The ceiling is pecky cypress," Baratta explains. "He loved wood — I'm sure the poor guy would be upset if he knew I painted over it! He traveled a lot and would bring back a board from each country, so there were all these different, wacky woods."

Although some of the wood is toned down, the house is about all that is decidedly not urban: Baratta blends his signature nautical themes with Adirondack furniture and Western/log cabin accessories. "It's a combination of the three places I love most: Maine, the Adirondacks, and the Hamptons," notes Baratta, whose firm has designed at least fifteen houses in eastern Long Island.

It's also a place to experiment. Baratta and his business partner, Bill Diamond, are well known for their bold, colorful, and offbeat interiors. While they have always had to rely

Above: An armchair at Baratta's Flanders house sports Lighthouse Print from the Diamond & Baratta collection for Lee Jofa. Right: Baratta painted the floor of the living room red, then overlaid it with a custom braided red rug. The aged armoire is mounted into a wall adorned with tramp art. A Diamond Baratta Design custom fabric adorns the sofa in the living room and in the sitting room. This lighthouse is from Baratta's collection.

182 ■

Below left: Bumper stickers add a touch of humor to the kitchen. Below right: Back on the screened porch, a trio of lighthouses stand sentinel. Opposite: Baratta covered a Victorian sofa in the living room with red Cape Lookout Weave from their Lee Jofa collection.

shelves hold hundreds of electric yellow *National Geographic* magazines. "It's not just for looks," he explains. "I have read *National Geographic* since the seventies. Actually, I just let the subscription lapse, and I've been feeling guilty about it."

Baratta's bedroom says "west" and "wild." "I lined the walls with exterior paneling from fake log-cabin siding," he says. Toy gun belts studded with rhinestones are hung like trophies. A three-foot-tall cowboy, complete with lasso, serves as a bedside lamp. "It was a water sprinkler, but the guy I bought it from said that if it didn't work, I could use it as a lamp."

Baratta resisted the urge to expand the house by not winterizing the wide porch. "This is a real, old-fashioned, screened-in porch. Although I only use it in the summer, I

wanted to keep it that way. It may sound like a small thing [to add glass panes], but it would really change the character of the house."

Here and there sit little lighthouses Baratta collects. As it turns out, even the collection is connected to the house. "My friends left their furniture here for a summer after I bought it, and there was a great little lighthouse. Then they took everything, and then I started collecting with the idea of getting that lighthouse back. Twenty years later, they gave it to me as surprise gift! Things happen in funny ways here in Flanders."

186 ■

SOURCES

The Hamptons is home to some of the finest garden centers, antiques shops, and home furnishings stores in the country, many of which will ship items anywhere in the world. This resource list is a guide to finding the products and materials featured in this book, with an emphasis on Hamptons sources — a great starting point for local explorations — though also incorporating some of our favorite sources in New York City and beyond. Note that some sources are open only to the trade; please call ahead before visiting.

Luxury and Home Stores

The American Wing
2415 Main St.
Bridgehampton, NY 11932
631-537-3319
www.theamericanwing.com

Amy Perlin Antiques
2462 Main St.
Bridgehampton, NY 11932
631-537-6161

Bagley Home
34 Main St.
Sag Harbor, NY 11963
631-725-3553

Balasses House Antiques
208 Main St.
Amagansett, NY 11930
631-267-3032

Battle Iron & Bronze
112 Maple Ln.
Bridgehampton, NY 11932
631-537-2193

Elegant John
74 Montauk Hwy.
East Hampton, NY 11937
631-324-2636

Fishers Home Furnishings
144 Main St.
Sag Harbor, NY 11963
631-725-0006

H Groome
9 Main St.
Southampton, NY 11968
631-204-0491

Hildreths's
51–55 Main St.
Southampton, NY 11968
631-283-2300

In Home
132 Main St.
Sag Harbor, NY 11963
631-725-7900

Inside Out
11 Railroad Ave.
East Hampton, NY 11937
631-329-3600

Jarlathdan
303 Main St.
Amagansett, NY 11930
631-267-6455

Tiffany & Co.
53 Main St.
East Hampton, NY 11937
631-324-1700

Antiques Stores

Ada's Attic
116 W. Montauk Hwy.
Hampton Bays, NY 11946
631-728-2141

Apsara Interior
74 Montauk Hwy.
East Hampton, NY 11937
631-329-3553

Architrove
74 Montauk Hwy.
East Hampton, NY 11937
631-329-2229

Another Time Antiques
765 Hill St.
Southampton, NY 11968
631-283-6223

Barbara Trujillo Kinnaman Ramaekers Kelter Malcé Antiques
2466 Main St.
Bridgehampton, NY 11932
631-537-3838

Barn 'arage
910 Montauk Hwy.
Water Mill, NY 11976
631-834-6897

Bloom
43 Madison St.
Sag Harbor, NY 11963
631-725-5940

Christian K. Andrews
7 Tradesman's Path
Bridgehampton, NY 11932
631-537-2877

Chez Soi
2426 Main St.
Bridgehampton, NY 11932
631-537-0496

Comerford Hennessy at Home
2442 Main St.
Bridgehampton, NY 11932
631-537-6200

Country Gear
2408 Main St.
Bridgehampton, NY 11932
631-537-1032

Croft Antiques
11 S. Main St.
Southampton, NY 11968
631-283-6445

Denton & Gardner
2491 Main St.
Bridgehampton, NY 11932
631-537-4796

Donna Parker
710 Montauk Hwy.
Water Mill, NY 11976
631-726-9311

English Country Antiques & Home Furnishings
26 Snake Hollow Rd.
Bridgehampton, NY 11932
631-537-0606

Gemini Antiques
2418 Main St.
Bridgehampton, NY 11932
631-537-4565

Georgica Creek Antiques
332 Montauk Hwy.
Wainscott, NY 11975
631-537-0333

Good Ground Antique Center
52 W. Montauk Hwy.
Hampton Bays, NY 11946
631-728-6300

Gray Gardens Antiques
Montauk Hwy. at Poxabogue Ln.
Bridgehampton, NY 11932
631-537-4848

Hampton Briggs Antiques
2462 Main St.
Bridgehampton, NY 11932
631-537-6286

Homenature
6 Main St.
Southampton, NY 11968
631-287-6277
and
255 Main St.
Amagansett, NY 11930
631-267-6647
www.homenature.com

J. Garvin Mecking
27 Washington St.
Sag Harbor, NY 11963
631-725-4932

Jonathan Adler
6 Main St. (mews)
East Hampton, NY 11937
631-329-6499
www.jonathanadler.com

John Salibello Antiques
2309 Main St.
Bridgehampton, NY 11932
631-537-1484
www.johnsalibelloantiques.com

Junk Yard Dog
2 Rose St.
Sag Harbor, NY 11963
631-725-3662

Lars Bolander
74 Montauk Hwy.
East Hampton, NY 11937
631-329-3400

Laurin Copen Antiques
1703 Montauk Hwy.
Bridgehampton, NY 11932
631-537-2802

Liza Sherman
112 Hampton St.
Sag Harbor, NY 11963
631-725-1437

LoCo
1 Main St.
East Hampton, NY 11937
631-907-9100

Mary Ann Lembo Antiques
97 School St.
Bridgehampton, NY 11932
631-537-9062

Mecox Gardens
257 County Rd. 39
Southampton, NY 11968
631-287-5015

Morgan MacWhinnie Antiques
1411 North Sea Rd.
Southampton, NY 11968
631-283-3366

Nellie's of Amagansett
230 Main St.
Amagansett, NY 11930
631-267-1000

Neo-Studio
25 Madison St.
Sag Harbor, NY 11963
631-725-6478

OPM Auction Gallery
5 Library Ave.
Westhampton, NY 11977
631-288-1850

Pritam & Eames
29 Race Ln.
East Hampton, NY 11937
631-324-7111

R. E. Steele Antiques
74 Montauk Hwy.
East Hampton, NY 11937
631-324-7812

Roark
7 Spring St.
Sag Harbor, NY 11963
631-725-7193

Sage Street Antiques
Sage St. & Route 114
Sag Harbor, NY 11963
631-725-4036

Sag Harbor Antiques Shop
17 Madison St.
Sag Harbor, NY 11963
631-725-1732

Schorr & Dobinsky
2491 Main St.
Bridgehampton, NY 11932
631-537-4635

Ted Meyer's Harbor Antiques
3654 Montauk Hwy.
Wainscott, NY 11975
631-537-1442

25 Hampton Road
25 Hampton Rd.
Southampton, NY 11968
631-287-3859

Walker Zabriskie
10 Job's Ln.
Southampton, NY 11968
631-283-5500

The Yard Couple
Bridge St. (off Rose St.)
Sag Harbor, NY 11963
631-725-7200

The Yard Sale
68 Newtown Ln.
East Hampton, NY 11937
631-324-7048

Youngblood
26 Madison St.
Sag Harbor, NY 11963
631-725-6260

Art Galleries

Boltax Gallery
21 N. Ferry Rd.
Shelter Island, NY 11964
631-749-4062
www.boltaxgallery.com

Gallery Merz
95 Main St.
Sag Harbor, NY 11963
631-725-2803

Glenn Horowitz Bookseller & Gallery
87 Newtown Ln.
East Hampton, NY 11937
631-324-5511

Mark Borghi
2442 Main St.
Bridgehampton, NY 11932
631-537-7245

Sara Nightingale Gallery
688 Montauk Hwy.
Water Mill, NY 11976
631-726-0076

Vered Gallery
68 Park Place Passage
East Hampton, NY 11937
631-324-3303

Garden Centers

Bayberry Home and Garden Center
Montauk Hwy.
Amagansett, NY 11930
631-267-3000

The Baywoods
910 Montauk Hwy.
Water Mill, NY 11976
631-726-5950

Buckley's Flowershop
75 Montauk Hwy.
East Hampton, NY 11937
631-324-0966

Country Gardens
Snake Hollow Rd.
Bridgehampton, NY 11932
631-537-0007

East Hampton Gardens
4 Gingerbread Ln.
East Hampton, NY 11937
631-324-1133

Liberty Farm Nursery
651 Main St.
Southampton, NY 11968
631-537-8001

Marders
Snake Hollow Rd.
Bridgehampton, NY 11932
631-537-3701

Spielberg Nursery & Garden Shop
500 Montauk Hwy.
East Hampton, NY 11937
631-329-1101

Topping's Greenhouse
109 Town Line Rd.
Sagaponack, NY 11962
631-537-4764

Warren's
779 Montauk Hwy.
Water Mill, NY 11976
631-726-4767

Wittendale's Florist and Greenhouses Inc.
89 Newtown Ln.
East Hampton, NY 11937
631-324-7160

Fabrics

Fabrics from the sources listed here are available through architects, interior designers, and other design professionals.

A. M. Collections
212-625-2616

Artmark
800-777-6665
www.artmarkfabrics.com

Bergamo
212-888-3333

Brunschwig & Fils
212-838-7878
www.brunschwig.com

Clarence House
800-221-4704
www.clarencehouse.com

Cowtan & Tout
212-753-4488

Donghia
800-366-4442
www.donghia.com

Edelman Leather
212-751-3339, 800-886-8339
www.edelmanleather.com

Fortuny
212-753-7153
www.fortuny.com

F. Schumacher & Co.
212-415-3900, 800-523-1200
www.fschumacher.com

Glant
800-88GLANT

Henry Calvin Fabric
541-732-1996, 888-732-1996
www.henrycalvin.com

Hinson and Co.
212-688-5538

Holly Hunt New York
212-755-6555
www.hollyhunt.com

J. Robert Scott
212-755-4910, 800-322-4910
www.jrobertscott.com

Jim Thompson Silk
800-262-0336

Kravet
800-645-9068
www.kravet.com

Larsen
212-753-4488

Lee Jofa
888-533-5632
www.leejofa.com

Nancy Corzine
212-223-8340

Old World Weavers
212-752-9000
www.starkcarpet.com

Ralph Lauren Home
888-475-7674
rlhome.polo.com

Rogers & Goffigon
212-888-3242

Rose Tarlow-Melrose House available at Holly Hunt
212-755-6555
www.hollyhunt.com

Scalamandré
212-980-3888
www.scalamandre.com

TylerGraphic available at John Rosselli
212-593-2060

Watkins & Fonthill
212-755-6700

Rugs and Floor Coverings

ABC Carpet and Home
888 Broadway
New York, NY 10003
212-473-3000
www.abchome.com

A. M. Collections
584 Broadway
New York, NY 10012
212-625-2616

Beauvais
201 E. 57th St.
New York, NY 10022
212-688-2265
www.beauvaiscarpets.com

Carini Lang
335 Greenwich St.
New York, NY 10013
646-613-0497
www.carinilang.com

Carpetman
633 County Rd. 39A
Southampton, NY 11968
631-283-0885

Country Carpet & Rug
207 Robbins Ln.
Syosset, NY 11791
516-822-5855
www.countrycarpet.com

Dolma Inc.
417 Lafayette St., 2nd Floor
New York, NY 10003
212-460-5525

Fort Street Studio
578 Broadway
New York, NY 10012
212-925-5383
www.fortstreetstudio.com

Misha Carpet
18 E. 53rd St.
New York, NY 10022
212-688-5912

The Nemati Collection
888-7-NEMATI
www.nematicollection.com

Odegard
200 Lexington Ave.
New York, NY 10016
212-545-0069
www.odegardcarpets.com

Patterson Flynn and Martin
212-688-7700, 212-213-7900

Stark Carpet
212-752-9000
www.starkcarpet.com

Additional Home Sources

Alan Court & Associates Inc.
34 Park Place
East Hampton, NY 11937
631-324-7497

Bob Stevens Appliances
Gabreski Airport Building 90
Westhampton Beach,
NY 11977
631-288-3000

Urban Archaeology
2231 Montauk Hwy.
Bridgehampton, NY 11932
631-537-0124
www.urbanarchaeology.com

Waterworks
87 Newtown Ln.
East Hampton, NY 11937
631-329-8201, 800-927-2120
www.waterworks.com

NEW YORK CITY STORES

ABC Carpet and Home
888 Broadway
New York, NY 10003
212-473-3000
www.abchome.com

Aero
419 Broome St.
New York, NY 10013
212-966-4700
www. aerostudios.com

Amy Perlin Antiques
306 E. 61st St.
New York, NY 10021
212-593-5756

Boffi
31½ Greene St.
New York, NY 10013
212-431-8282
www.boffi.com

Janus et Cie
221 E. 59th St.
New York, NY 10022
212-752-1117, 800-24Janus
www.janusetcie.com

Interieurs
151 Franklin St.
New York, NY 10013
212-343-0800

Kartell
39 Greene St.
New York, NY 10013
212-966-6665

■ 189

INDEX

CREDITS

Writers

Fred Bernstein (Temporary Contemporary, p. 104)

Marina Isola Campbell (Chez Ginsberg, p. 20; Building with the Past, p. 72; Camp Baratta, p. 180)

Barbara Dixon (An Endless Summer, p. 36)

Stephen Henderson (House and Gardener, p. 96; Lilliputian Manor, p. 88; La Bella Casa, p. 132; The Art of Living, p. 164; Play House, p. 172)

Donna Paul (Above the Maddening Crowds, p. 28; Rooms with a View, p. 112)

Ellen Sherman (Gilding the Lily, p. 60)

Lockhart Steele (Dune Maneuvers, p. 12; Rainbow in a Box, p. 80; At Home with the Past, p. 140)

Newell Turner (Spellbound, p. 44; Bay Watch, p. 52; Blockbuster, p. 120; In the Eye of the Beholder, p. 148; American Anthem, p. 156)

Photographers

Tria Giovan (Temporary Contemporary, p. 104; The Art of Living, p. 164)

Michael Grimm (Above the Maddening Crowds, p. 28; Rainbow in a Box, p. 80; Lilliputian Manor, p. 88; Play House, p. 172)

Steve Gross & Sue Daley (At Home with the Past, p. 140)

John Hall (Bay Watch, p. 52; Rooms with a View, p. 112); also pp. 6, 8, 11, 68, and 128

Alec Hemer (Dune Maneuvers, p. 12)

Laurie Lambrecht (An Endless Summer, p. 36; House and Gardener, p. 96; La Bella Casa, p. 132)

Joshua McHugh (American Anthem, p. 156)

Gary McLeod (In the Eye of the Beholder, p. 148)

Bärbel Miebach (Spellbound, p. 44; Blockbuster, p. 120)

Laura Resen (Camp Baratta, p. 180)

Kim Sargent (Building with the Past, p. 72)

Loyal Sewell (Gilding the Lily, p. 60)

Karin Willis (Chez Ginsberg, p. 20)

Thank You

Thanks to Dianne Benson, Kyle Blood, Beth Rudin DeWoody, Barbaralee Diamonstein-Spielvogel, Barbara Dixon, Sophie Donelson, Eileen Ekstract, Richard Ekstract, Sharon King Hoge, Barbara Kurgan, Lys Marigold, Ivy Tashlik, Jill Tashlik, Justin Troust, and the many gifted writers and photographers who regularly enliven the pages of *HC&G*. The introductory section essays by Amy Gross, Spalding Gray, and Rona Jaffe first appeared in *HC&G*, "The Real Hamptons," June 1, 2003. Thanks to the writers for agreeing to have their essays reprinted here.

On the Web

You can visit *Hamptons Cottages & Gardens* on the web at www.HCandG.com.